THE BEATLES
FAB BUT TRUE
Remarkable Stories Revealed

DOUG WOLFBERG | Foreword by Tom Frangione

THE **BEATLES**
FAB BUT TRUE
Remarkable Stories Revealed

DOUG WOLFBERG

Foreword by Tom Frangione

SCHIFFER
PUBLISHING

4880 Lower Valley Road · Atglen, PA 19310

OTHER SCHIFFER BOOKS ON RELATED SUBJECTS

Copyright © 2023 by Doug Wolfberg

Library of Congress Control Number: 2023931144

Designed by Christopher Bower
Cover design by Christopher Bower
Type set in Arboria/Baskerville
ISBN: 978-0-7643-6683-3
Printed in China

Published by Schiffer Publishing, Ltd.
4880 Lower Valley Road
Atglen, PA 19310
Phone: (610) 593-1777; Fax: (610) 593-2002
Email: Info@schifferbooks.com
Web: www.schifferbooks.com

For our complete selection of fine books on this and related subjects, please visit our website at www.schifferbooks.com. You may also write for a free catalog.

Schiffer Publishing's titles are available at special discounts for bulk purchases for sales promotions or premiums. Special editions, including personalized covers, corporate imprints, and excerpts, can be created in large quantities for special needs. For more information, contact the publisher.

We are always looking for people to write books on new and related subjects. If you have an idea for a book, please contact us at proposals@schifferbooks.com.

FSC
www.fsc.org
MIX
Paper | Supporting
responsible forestry
FSC® C104723

For my wife, Tina, who makes it all worthwhile.

CONTENTS

FOREWORD

Now everybody seems to have their own opinion,
Who did this and who did that.
But as for me I don't see how they can remember,
When they weren't where it was at.
—Paul McCartney ("Early Days," 2013)

As the Beatles crossed the plane from "World's Biggest Band" into the history books in 1970 (and, to an equal or greater extent, one decade later), their legacy called for a scholarly approach to documenting their story. Birthdates, favorite colors, and hobbies as chronicled in the teen magazines of the 1960s would hardly suffice as the historical record.

Around this time, "serious" rock journalism was taking shape in the offices of *Rolling Stone* and other outlets. Going forward, things might be viewed with a more critical eye, but what about the past? Thus was born the era of the Beatles "scholars." Their work in digging through print, audio, film, and other archives has been a boon to Beatles fans and collectors for nearly fifty years now.

I don't ask for a lot (and boy do I get it!), but I really like for things to make sense. And while I never even applied to detective school, I love a good forensic exercise. More specifically, I love to watch other people do the forensic exercises and learn from them. One of the earliest such exercises was published in *Stereo Review* magazine back in 1977, "The Case of the Belittled Beatles Tapes" by Harry Castleman and Wally Podrazik. I won't spoil it for you (you can find it online), but suffice it to say their work trumped the collective efforts of the Beatles' own legal team and could have saved them decades of heartache and a small fortune in attorneys' fees.

The ensuing years saw the pioneering work of truly elite researchers, writers, and historians, such as Mark Lewisohn and Kevin Howlett. Their work in piecing together and documenting the Beatles' studio and BBC recordings was truly a watershed effort for which every Beatles fan and collector owes a debt of gratitude that could never, ever be repaid.

And meanwhile, back at the ranch, the biographies that chronicled the band's history—sometimes objectively and sometimes not—relied on the loosest of "facts," handed-down folklore, conjecture, and, even worse, generational skimping, misinterpretation, and cutting of corners in the veracity department, coming off as a poorly played version of that old game "Telephone."

Modern-day researchers, historians, and writers are thus faced with two hills to climb: debunking the long-ingrained "truths" and then (and only then) setting the record straight.

To be fair to everyone—even the guy whose lyrics I quoted at the top of this foreword—a lot of the Beatles' history is sixty years of age or more. Even the best memories can fade over that many decades. Moreover, you can bet that for someone (say, Paul McCartney himself) who was busy living those experiences, documenting, archiving, and journalizing things was usually an afterthought, at best. Living these dreams, fueling their creativity, and making the history were certainly more at the forefront.

So even Paul, who was there (full disclosure, I wasn't) on September 10, 1963, when the Beatles "gave" the Rolling Stones a song to record, tells the story (one told in full in chapter 6) with a couple of major holes in it. We love Paul and forgive him such transgressions, of course. While it may "embellish" things and make for an easier telling of the story, those side steps from the fact pattern only stoke the fires that historians are trying to extinguish.

Which, quite paradoxically, is why discussing that particular story with one of the beneficiaries, Rolling Stones bassist Bill Wyman, was a most welcome opportunity when he was our guest on the Fab Fourum over at the Beatles Channel on SiriusXM. You see, Bill is of that rare breed of megastar and someone who notoriously served as the band's unofficial archivist. Check out his book *Rolling with the Stones* and the documentary film *The Quiet One* for great examples of how to simultaneously document and be part of the same experience.

So, yes, Sir Paul, you are correct. I wasn't there. Neither were any of the scholars I've mentioned here, nor this book's author, Doug Wolfberg. But, with forensic skills that would make Sherlock Holmes, Sam Spade, Sergeant Friday, Charlie Chan, and Peter Gunn all green with envy, Doug has drilled deep into some stories that have heretofore been somewhat hazy on details and that, before now, left us with more questions than answers along the way.

Upon meeting Doug, I kicked the tires a bit and sought some fleshed-out answers surrounding the great "Roots" debacle John Lennon endured in the mid-1970s. Way beyond the diligence he clearly performed (you'll see what I'm talking about when you get to chapter 12), I found that his knowledge of Beatles history was matched only by his enthusiasm and passion for them.

And while most of my own Beatles reading these days takes the form of reference books, it's refreshing to find a book such as *Fab but True*—part reference, but in a narrative style that serves the band's incredible story with the color and "How about that!" surprises we first experienced via the Beatles' music, before we ever read our first biography of them.

And so, the book you hold in your hands will no doubt shed some light and additional perspective on some stories you might already feel you have enough information about. Trust me. You don't.

I'm thankful to Doug for our newfound friendship and collegiality, and the honor of being asked to preview the manuscript and to serve as something of a sounding board, and the privilege of introducing the book to you, dear reader. There'll be no quiz at the end, but you'll be well suited to be the life of the party the next time the Beatles come up in conversation, or at the next Beatles convention that you attend, which I hope is soon.

Tom Frangione
Scotch Plains, New Jersey
2023

PREFACE

The world is a crowded bookshelf of Beatles books. Yet, *Fab but True* endeavors to fill a niche and a need that has not yet been met. That is, to offer a forensic deep dive into fascinating characters and compelling backstories behind some of the most remarkable events in the Beatles' history.

Along with our four main protagonists, these stories bring to life a colorful cast that includes a mobster, a flamboyant lawyer, a duplicitous concert promoter, a free-spirited Liverpudlian housewife, a long-shot racehorse, a couple of anonymous drummers, and a gentle giant, among other captivating characters. Their stories range from the cosmically implausible (Paul coincidentally conjuring up a fictional name shared by a long-dead woman who lies beneath the soil of the very place he and John first met) to the whimsical (the flaming condom that got two Beatles deported from Germany) to the downright tragic (the sad ending of a Beatles roadie and confidant who served them quietly and loyally for virtually their entire career).

Myths can subsume legends. Readers may be surprised at the ways some of these stories differ in key respects from that which has emerged over the hazy decades of Beatles lore. This book aspires to bring those stories back to their factual moorings.

The stories I selected for this book run the gamut from the familiar to the more obscure. While some of the stories are better known than others, readers might not be as familiar with the extraordinarily rich depth of these events and the central players involved. These chapters provide a fuller context and aim to restore forgotten facts of these captivating stories. Each chapter tells a central story, followed by a postscript that tells the story after the story. In many cases, these afterwords are as fascinating and dramatic as the central stories themselves.

Although this book was extensively researched, cites multiple sources (both current and contemporaneous), and is, I hope, entirely factual, it is not intended as a scholarly work of history. Other researchers and writers (some of whom showed me great kindness in this effort) have made outstanding contributions in that regard. I am indebted to the dedication and diligence of the academic Beatles historians. Still, doing deep dives on sometimes obscure events a half century or more after they took place poses challenges. Although I list in the acknowledgments the names of many who have helped me, any errors in these pages are mine and mine alone.

Another goal I kept in the forefront of my mind with every tap of the keyboard was to tell these stories in a way that would raise the eyebrows of Beatles superfans, delight casual fans, and enlighten Beatles newcomers. If I've even come close to threading that needle, I will consider my work a success. That is now for you, the reader, to decide.

Camp Hill, Pennsylvania
2023

ACKNOWLEDGMENTS

Writing a book is no solitary effort. I am deeply indebted to everyone whose names are listed here for making contributions to this work.

One of the amazing things I found about writing a book about the Beatles is that people who have already written books or other projects about the Beatles are generous in sharing their time, research, insight, expertise, suggestions, and images. Distinguished authors and producers to whom I owe my deepest appreciation include Kenneth Womack, Chuck Gunderson, David Bedford, and Simon Weitzman.

When one has a deep, abiding, and lifelong love of the Beatles, there's nothing quite like hearing firsthand stories of people who were there. I am grateful to these notable individuals who have over the years shared with me firsthand accounts of the Beatles and their associates: Rory Best, Geoff Emerick (RIP), Tony Bramwell, and original Quarryman Rod Davis.

Beatles experts who shared their expertise or words and for whom I am deeply appreciative include Mark Lapidos and Frank Caiazzo. Undying thanks also to musicians extraordinaire Gregg Bissonette and Billy J. Kramer.

To my family and friends who either traveled with me to visit Beatles sites, or to meet Beatle people, or who simply endured endless hours of Beatles stories, thank you. This long-suffering lot includes my kids, Josh, Cayla and Sophie Wolfberg; my siblings, Mark Wolfberg, Jeff Wolfberg, and Melissa Frye; and friends Tim Perkins, Dave Lutz, Karl Januzzi, Jim Goldsmith, and Steve Wirth.

An enormous thank-you to those who helped me with the process of building a book, such as development, editing, indexing, image rights, the publishing process, and overall support. These indispensable people include Nancy Peterson, Sheri Polley, Theresa Davis, David Meerman Scott, Susan Turley, and everyone at Schiffer Publishing, notably publisher Pete Schiffer and editor Bob Biondi.

My deepest thanks to a man who gets his own category: Tom Frangione, who in 2020 answered the unsolicited email of a guy he didn't know and then became a good friend. Tom opened doors, facilitated introductions, provided technical advice, wrote a foreword, served as a sounding board, shared images from his personal collection, and made me write an extra chapter after I—apparently prematurely—thought I'd finished writing. Chapter 6 is for you, buddy!

My warmest gratitude is reserved for my wife, Tina Wolfberg, for her encouragement, support, tolerance, and love. Finally, thanks to our adopted dog, Lucy, who spent many hours on my lap or at my feet during extended research and writing sessions (she put in almost as many hours as I), and the many rescued cats with Beatle-related names who prowl our house and hiss their words of support. At least I choose to believe that constitutes support.

Please consider rescuing a pet or supporting a reputable animal rescue organization near you.

CHAPTER 1

NEVER SAY DIE
How a Racehorse Helped Save the Beatles

Never Say Die was an American-bred horse set to compete in the 1954 running of the prestigious Derby Stakes. The longest of long shots, with 33:1 odds—history can draw a straight line from this colt's improbable victory to the launch of the Beatles. This is the incredible story of how a horse race helped save the world's biggest band. From the 1954 Derby, we fast-forward to the summer of 1959 to begin this fab tale.

In the summer of 1959, the musical dreams of John, Paul, and George were going nowhere fast.

Before the Beatles became, well, *the Beatles*, they were teenagers in working-class Liverpool, not long out of school and stuck at the crossroads that every young band encounters. At that intersection of Normalcy Lane to the right and Stardom Drive to the left, the majority of bands turn right and take the safe path to a "normal" life. Get a job, maybe attend college, get married, have a family—be *sensible*, for heaven's sake. Pick up your guitar or play your drums occasionally just to remember that you can. Some of the musicians marching down this well-worn path might become weekend warriors, playing in local bands in local clubs for local crowds, and at least getting to experience a minute, fleeting sense of life under the lights.

What of the few, the daring, the truly *senseless* bands that decide to turn left and take the other road? They most often face a future of despair, hardship, and dues-paying deprivation. As soon as they make that turn, they must hustle for paying gigs, exposure, and traction in an indifferent world. Only a very few bands will ever "make it," and it takes a special, slightly delusional audacity to think yours will. From the hindsight of a half century, we know how this choice turned out for the Beatles. However, like every aspiring band, there was a time when their very survival was far from ensured.

So it was for the Beatles in the summer of 1959. Of course, they were not yet known as the Beatles. John and Paul, who were later joined by George and a few others who came and went, called themselves the Quarrymen, after the Quarry Bank High School that John had attended. John was eighteen, Paul was seventeen, and George was just sixteen (and a recent high school dropout). Just the right age and stage for their parents (in John's case, his guardian, his maternal Aunt Mimi) to begin exerting pressure to get jobs or continue their schooling. To start their independent, adult lives. To get the hell out of my house, as a war-weary, 1950s Liverpudlian parent might put it.

Paid gigs were hard to come by. In fact, the Quarrymen had not had one in months. John had been working as a laborer, hauling bricks and working on construction sites. By his own admission, he was not doing a particularly good job of it. Paul was delivering furniture for a local department store and working at an electric-coil factory. George wasn't doing much of anything, except playing part-time in a band called the Les Stewart Quartet. But Les and the others in the quartet were standing at the same crossroads at the same time as the Quarrymen. Under similar pressure from similarly impatient parents, they chose college, work, and normalcy. So, George, too, was left without a gig and with no prospects.

It is hard to overstate for the history of music and Western culture just how pivotal the summer of '59 was for John, Paul, and George, standing as they were at this decisive intersection of their lives. Add to this mix the fact that their intersection was in Liverpool—*Liverpool*—the north of England, or the "provinces," as they were disdainfully labeled by Londoners and the metropolitans. *Nobody* in popular music had come from there. The prevailing belief in English society at this time was that there was no talent to be found in these blue-collar, uneducated, uncultured, primitive hinterlands. The path to musical stardom was simply not previously available to lowly Liverpudlians.

This summer of '59 was determinative for John, Paul, and George. No doubt the words "never say die" crossed their minds. But they could have had no way of knowing just how important that phrase would be to their futures and, by extension, the future of the 1960s and the whole damn twentieth century.

From here, we rewind to the spring of 1954. It's a chilly, misty, wet day in Epsom, Surrey, about 30 miles southwest of London. If you have ever taken a relaxing soak in Epsom salts, you well know the spa-like minerals originally harvested in this area.

The Derby Stakes was—and continues to be—one of the premier horse races in England (though it is now also known as the Cazoo Derby, owing to its current sponsorship by a British online automobile retailer). One of the legs of the British Triple Crown, it has been run annually since 1780 on the first Saturday of June. On June 2, 1954, nearly a quarter-million spectators, including Her Majesty the Queen, packed into the galleries of the storied racetrack, Epsom Downs, to see the spectacle and hear the hoofbeats.

British jockey Lester Piggott atop Never Say Die at the 1954 Epsom Derby. *Photo: George W. Hales / Fox Photos / Getty Images*

The 1954 edition of "the Derby" included a rather unusual entry. An *American*-bred, three-year-old colt named Never Say Die—named for a near-death experience at birth—was entered by its American owner Robert Sterling Clark. Clark was an heir to the Singer Sewing Machine fortune. Riding the number 5 chestnut colt was as-yet-unheralded jockey Lester Piggott. No American-owned, American-bred filly or colt had ever won the Derby, so Never Say Die was a 33-to-1 long shot—the horse judged by oddsmakers as the least likely to win.

A striking image of young Mona Best serves as the backdrop for her sons Pete and Roag, December 2018. *Photo: ANL/Shutterstock*

Listening to the race on BBC Radio in Liverpool, 220 miles northwest of Surrey, was thirty-year-old Mona Best. An exotic beauty in an unhappy marriage, Mona was raised in privilege in Madras (now Chennai), India. She was a free spirit who refused to submit to her domineering husband, the well-known Liverpool boxing promoter Johnny Best. Mona craved independence for herself and her young children, Pete and Rory. To get it, she took the audacious step of pawning her valuable jewelry and betting all the proceeds in the 1954 Derby on Never Say Die, the longest of long shots. Why Never Say Die? She later said that she simply liked the name and thought it perfectly captured her spirit.

Shockingly, Never Say Die pulled away in the final quarter of the race, never relinquishing his two-length lead. As the BBC announced his victory, Mona literally jumped for joy. She paid the ransom to retrieve her jewelry, leaving a tidy sum with which to reclaim her independence.

Despite her husband's objections, or perhaps because of them, Mona had her eye on a rundown, fifteen-room Victorian house at number 8 Hayman's Green in a leafy Liverpool suburb called West Derby. Formerly the headquarters

The Best home, Hayman's Green, West Derby, Liverpool. *Photo: Doug Wolfberg*

of the West Derby Conservative Club, the large house had fallen on hard times. But Mona spied potential in the stately manor. With the winnings from the improbable victory of her champion Never Say Die, she placed a sizable down payment on the property, and it became hers in 1957.

Mona had seen a TV show about a coffee club for teenagers in London, which sparked her idea to set up a gathering place in the large, multiple-room basement. Here, her teenage boys and their friends, along with Liverpool's other music-starved youth, could see live bands in a safe, controlled environment. The club would not serve alcohol, and no drugs would be permitted. Its only stimulants were music and the caffeine in the espresso from the coffee bar, which was often staffed by her younger son, Rory.

Inspired by the walled-in capital city in the movie *Algiers*, Mona named her club the Casbah Coffee Club.

After renovating the house to her satisfaction, Mona scheduled the opening of the Casbah for August 29, 1959. Club memberships were sold—blue cards for boys and pink for girls—and a large turnout was expected for the opening.

Mona originally booked the Les Stewart Quartet for what, at the time, seemed to be a wholly inauspicious event. Alas, its other three members had landed "safe" jobs and given up their musical pursuits, so the band was no longer available. The resourceful George Harrison, the high school dropout desperate to avoid a consignment to normalcy, suggested to Mona that he and his friends John and Paul, along with fellow Quarryman Ken Brown, provide the entertainment for the opening. John and Paul jumped at the chance. Mona conceded, telling the boys that if it went well, they could have a regular residency at the club. A paid, recurring gig! At a time when their musical prospects seemed to be drying up, this was precisely the lifeline the budding band needed.

The opening of the Casbah offered an unexpected resuscitation of the flailing fortunes of the newly christened Quarrymen. If ever there was a right time and a right place, the summer of 1959 and the Casbah were it for the soon-to-be Beatles.

For the next few months, the Casbah became the glue that held the newly invigorated Quarrymen together, and it kept John, Paul, and George bound in each other's orbits. Mona acted as a manager for the resurgent band, helping them book paying gigs at other local venues, including the Cavern Club in Liverpool. It wasn't much, but compared with the drought they had experienced in the summer of 1959, it was enough.

About seven weeks into their Casbah residency, John, Paul, and George fell out with Mona over money. It seems Mona paid Ken Brown an equal share of the payment for a gig, even though he was sick and sat out the show in an upstairs room in the Best home. The lads stormed out, insisting they would never play the Casbah again. (Don't worry; they did. Read on, gentle reader.) Thus began a curious dance between the Best family and the Beatles, who would never fully distance themselves from one another, despite the rupture of their most-obvious ties.

Around this time, Mona's eldest son, Pete, acquired a drum kit and began to play with a local outfit called the Blackjacks. As fate would have it, an even more lucrative opportunity presented itself to John, Paul, and George in the summer of 1960: a promoter wanted a five-piece rock-and-roll band for a club residency in Hamburg, Germany. It would be hard work, playing for hours on end, seven days a week. But the young, hungry band—now known as the Beatles—grabbed the opportunity. Over the years, the Beatles had struggled to find a permanent drummer who had a complete kit and was reliable enough to show up for gigs. They often relied on the guitars to keep the beat; "The rhythm's in the guitars" was the answer they gave promoters who proved skeptical when they showed up drummerless. Remembering that Mona's son Pete owned a drum kit (a rare, expensive instrument in those days), Paul was deputized to reach out and gauge Pete's interest in the Hamburg gig. After Pete confirmed his interest, the others arranged a hasty audition. In short order, the band and its gear were headed to Germany.

Along with John, Paul, George, and bassist Stu Sutcliffe, Mona's son Pete filled out the five-piece band that arrived in Hamburg in August 1960 to fulfill their rendezvous with history (chapter 2 tells the story about how their first Hamburg residency ended in ignominy). Pete would sit on the Beatles' drum throne for the next two years (almost to the day), until . . . well, that's another story altogether.

In 1962, Mona was pregnant with her third child and her mother passed away. According to Pete, life simply became too hectic, and Mona could not keep up with the demands of family life while running the Casbah.

The story of Mona Best and the child she bore in 1962 is another fascinating though relatively unheralded tale in Beatles history. In addition to the gigs she provided at the Casbah and her early management of the band, Mona's house was one of the central gathering points for Liverpool's young rockers, even when there wasn't a show going on in the basement. Mona identified with the younger crowd, felt comfortable in their presence, and drew a certain freedom and vitality from her sons' contemporaries.

One of Pete's closest friends was Neil Aspinall. Mona was drawn to Neil, and the feeling was mutual. In 1961, Neil, then nineteen, and Mona, thirty-seven, began a romantic affair. Mona's pregnancy could no longer be hidden by 1962, and in July her son Roag was born. Although Johnny Best knew he was not the father, the child was given the Best surname to avoid a Liverpool suburban scandal. Johnny ultimately gave Mona an ultimatum to end her affair with Neil, but, as you can guess, Mona was not the type of woman who responded well to ultimatums from domineering men.

Johnny Best moved out shortly after his demand was rebuffed by his estranged wife.

Pete Best with his mother, Mona, after his dismissal from the Beatles.
Photo: John Smart / ANL / Shutterstock

After Pete's dismissal from the band in 1962, Neil labored over a tough choice: he could continue his service to the Beatles, whom everyone sensed were "going places," or quit out of loyalty to the Bests. Upon the urging both of Pete and Mona, Neil stayed on as the Beatles' driver, bridging the duality of their explosive worldwide success while remaining tied to the Best family and its dejected Beatle castoff.

Despite some bitterness held by Mona and Pete, the other Beatles did not completely sever their contact with the Bests. Although Pete was never again to speak to any of the Beatles (other than banalities in passing at local gigs), Mona helped them on occasion over the years. In fact, the war medals pinned to John's coat on the cover of *Sgt. Pepper's Lonely Hearts Club Band* belonged to Mona's father, and Mona lent them to John specifically for the cover shoot.

June 24, 1962, was the last show at the Casbah Coffee Club. That night's entertainment? The Beatles—now a four-piece band, with John and George on guitars, Paul on bass, and Pete on drums. They had returned to the Casbah after their inglorious walkout three years earlier.

It turns out that the Beatles had really cut their teeth in their Hamburg residencies. The mediocre, wannabe music outfit had become a seasoned, polished rock-and-roll band, complete with an impressive repertoire and a stage presence that was charming new fans. The Beatles was now a tight unit that packed a potent, reinvigorated punch.

So, John, Paul, and George—first as the Quarrymen and then as the Beatles—were the bookends of the Casbah's storied history as a coffee club and music venue from August 1959 to June 1962. But the summer 1959 gig in the Casbah, purchased with the winnings of a fortuitous wager, gave John, Paul, and George a life-sustaining gig—and a lucky bet on a lucky horse to thank for it.

POSTSCRIPT

Lester Piggott, who rode Never Say Die to victory in the Derby, went on to win many more races at Epsom and became a legend in British horse racing. He died in 2022. Never Say Die later commanded princely stud fees.

In 2018, Roag Best opened the Liverpool Beatles Museum (originally called the Magical Beatles Museum), mere steps from the site of the Cavern Club on Liverpool's storied Matthew Street. Much of the Beatles memorabilia that remained in the Best family can be seen there.

Neil Aspinall became the Beatles' driver, shuttling the increasingly busy and popular band to gigs in a beat-up van Mona had bought them. Given Neil and Pete's close friendship and later familial ties, Neil was a natural fit for the Beatle's circle in those early years.

After the band's touring years ended, Neil became their de facto manager after the death of Brian Epstein, and eventually the head of Apple Records. Neil is discussed in more detail in chapter 16.

Mona Best died in 1988. The house on Hayman's Green remains in the family. Although it is not open for tours on a regular schedule, fans can arrange tours through some of the in-the-know tour guides on the Liverpool circuit. Several factors make a tour of the Casbah far and away one of the best Beatles experiences in the world.

First, tours are given in small, intimate groups, often led by a member of the Best family or people whose history is tied to the Bests and the house. On my first tour, I was lucky enough to be guided by Rory Best, Mona's second son and an eyewitness to those formative years and some of the critical events in early Beatles history. He told firsthand stories while taking me and my friends through the Casbah cellar, patiently answering questions and posing for pictures. It was an extraordinary opportunity to hear from a direct witness to such momentous events as the Beatles hearing themselves on the radio for the first time, and John and Paul browbeating Stu into buying a bass and joining the band.

The author with Rory Best in the Spider Room of the Casbah, April 2016. *Photo: Doug Wolfberg*

The second reason the Casbah is an unrivaled Beatles heritage site is because its painted walls and ceilings have been preserved intact, as vivid and colorful as they were in 1959. This condition is thanks to the club's location in a basement with no natural light sources to degrade it over time. To help Mona get the club ready for its opening, the eager Quarrymen had painted the basement rooms in a variety of motifs—Aztec themes, a rainbow room, a ceiling of painted silver stars, a dragon, and a spider, not to mention surreptitious etchings by John Lennon as he carved his name into a wall. As a collective work of art by the Beatles (who were also talented visual artists), the walls and ceilings of the Casbah are the Sistine Chapel of Beatledom.

The third reason the Casbah is an irreplaceable, must-see mecca for Beatles fans is that it is the real McCoy. Many fans who make Beatles pilgrimages to Liverpool are disappointed to learn that the Cavern Club is but a replica of the original. Today's reproduction Cavern Club shares part of the footprint of the original club; although it is an important (and fun) Beatles site, the original was demolished in the 1970s. There is something profound about touching the same walls, seeing the same stage, and trodding on the same floor as the Beatles that gets lost in the replica. The Casbah is all original. It might not be the best-known Beatles site in Liverpool, but it happened there before it happened at the Cavern, and it happened at what was arguably the most critical time in the survival of the band that became the Beatles.

Without the Casbah, who knows how fate might have intervened in other places and other ways to keep John, Paul, and George together. The planets aligned in the summer of 1959, when their survival as a band was probably at its most tenuous, with the Casbah seeing to it that these indispensable musicians stayed together, and their band lived to fight another day. All made possible by a horse—and a strong woman.

Thank you, Mona.

CHAPTER 2

BETTER TO BURN OUT
How a Flaming Condom Got the Beatles Deported

In November 1960, the Beatles were in their first club residency in Hamburg, Germany. They lived in the filthy, rundown backrooms of the Bambi Kino, a second-run theater attached to their second-rate club. Even though they were under contract to the club's owner, a stocky German tough guy named Bruno Koschmider, the Beatles set their sights on a better gig at a more popular, competing club. They packed their belongings to make a late-night escape from Bruno's clutches and on to greener pastures. On their way out, Paul and Pete pulled a prank that led to their arrest and deportation from Germany, and the incident threatened to derail the Beatles' burgeoning career.

The brief stint of gigs at the Casbah in 1959 improved the Beatles' fortunes enough to continue to resist their parents' insistent demands to get "real" jobs. But, alas, 1960 did not prove to be much more successful than was 1959.

An audition for promoter Larry Parnes landed the Beatles (known for this brief period as the Silver Beetles) a gig on a short tour of Scotland, playing with singer Johnny Gentle. But soon after, their hard-won momentum fizzled, and they ended up right back in Liverpool in the all-too-familiar position of confronting slim prospects.

Then, once again, *das Schicksal*—or fate, as we say in English—intervened in the summer of 1960.

Allan Williams, described by Paul as a "small bloke" with a high-pitched Welsh voice and by George as "Liverpool's first groupie," had by this time become the Beatles' manager. According to Paul, Allan was "a good motivator . . . very good for us at the time."

Sometime around August 8, Allan took a call from German club owner Bruno Koschmider and his translator. Allan had fulfilled Bruno's earlier

From left, early Beatles' manager Allan Williams; his wife, Beryl; Liverpool singer and businessman Lord Wodbine; Stuart Sutcliffe; Paul McCartney; George Harrison; and Pete Best stopping at the Arnhem Oosterbeek War Cemetery in Netherlands, en route to their first Hamburg club residency, August 16, 1960. *Photo: Keystone Features / Getty Images*

requests to export British bands to his club in Hamburg to *mach schau* (make a show) and entertain his rowdy, hard-drinking patrons with live rock and roll. Bruno needed another British band for a new club he was opening near the city's seedy Reeperbahn district. Specifically, Bruno wanted a five-piece band for a two-month residency at his new club, the Indra.

As was customary, the club owner would provide his resident band with living accommodations.

Bruno Koschmider, proprietor of the Indra and Kaiserkeller clubs, in an undated photo. The theater behind him, Knopf's Lichtspielhaus, closed in 1965, so this image was likely taken before then. *Photo: Schaffrath / ullstein bild / Getty Images*

Bruno was impatient to open his new club and told Allan that he would need a band on stage and ready to rock in just one week. That was not much time for five members of a band to get their papers and plans in order, travel to Germany, and hit the stage. Unless, of course, it was a band that had a lot of downtime on their hands. On that score, the Beatles fit the bill.

However, Allan offered the new Indra residency to at least three other bands before the Beatles were called off the bench. Those bands, busier and less desperate than the Beatles, did not find it necessary to jump at a gig in Hamburg on a week's notice. So, finally, Allan offered the gig to the Beatles, who always seemed to be standing by waiting for *something* to happen. The Beatles jumped at the chance.

The only problem was that the Beatles at this point were only a four-piece band—John, Paul, and George on guitars and Stu Sutcliffe on bass. But Bruno wanted a five-piece band. Apparently, he had had good results with other five-piece bands; they could presumably *mach* 20 percent more *schau* than their four-piece counterparts. For the Beatles, finding a permanent and reliable drummer had been elusive. Although Paul filled in behind the kit as needed, and other drummers would take the throne on short notice, this was not a viable or reliable long-term solution.

Remembering that Mona Best's son Pete, whom they had met at the Casbah (see chapter 1), owned a drum kit and had been playing with another local band, the Blackjacks, the Beatles asked him to join them in Hamburg. This was very much an acquisition borne of necessity. As John put it, "We got Pete because we needed a drummer the next day to go to Hamburg."

A hasty "audition" was arranged for Pete, but not at the Casbah. They were still gun-shy about seeing Mona after running out on her over a financial dispute. This tryout would take place at one of the clubs owned by Allan Williams.

Although this session is commonly referred to as an "audition," the reality was that the boys were in no position to be picky about a drummer. This entire adventure probably consisted of no more than laying eyes on the lad behind the kit to make sure, in John's words, that "he could keep a stick moving up and down."

The now-five-piece band was ready to go. Shortly before embarking, the Silver Beetles changed their name to the Beatles. The decision was inspired by Buddy Holly's band, the Crickets, and the play on "beat" music, as rock and roll was known in the British clubs.

On August 16, 1960, nearly a year to the day after their lifesaving gig at the opening of the Casbah, the Beatles loaded up Allan's green Austin van and set out on the long trek to Hamburg.

Hamburg in 1960 was known as a seedy city of sex, drugs, and rock and roll. It hosted a rough-and-tumble mix of gangsters, prostitutes, strippers, and cross-dressers. According to Paul, the five young musicians were "let off the leash" for the first time. George later recalled that "everything was such a buzz, being right in the middle of the naughtiest city in the world at seventeen years-old . . . it was kind of exciting." Paul remarked that as kids who had little sexual experience before reaching Hamburg, meeting up with the "hard-core striptease artists" who obviously knew a thing or two about sex was "quite an eye-opener."

Although they had not yet discovered the condom's flammable qualities, the Beatles surely had a ready supply at their disposal to take full advantage of their newfound status as lads unleashed.

Less than twenty-four hours after their late-night arrival in Hamburg, the Beatles took the stage at the Indra club, beginning an uninterrupted, forty-eight-night slugfest of six-to-seven-hour nights. The long gigs forced the Beatles to expand their repertoire and develop a style and a stage presence. When they eventually returned to Liverpool, people were shocked at what a tight, rocking band the former Quarrymen / Silver Beetles had become.

Bruno had assured Allan that he would provide accommodations to his new resident band. Maybe the German did not translate well into English, but "accommodations," they would soon learn, was a pretty loose term.

On August 17, 1960, the four young men who would go on to become among the most influential and wealthiest musicians of their time were led down a corridor to two filthy storage rooms in the back of a theater attached to the club. The theater was called the Bambi-Filmkunsttheater (the Bambi Film Art Theater), known as the Bambi Kino (cinema). Although later accounts portray the Bambi Kino as a porno theater, it was not. It featured mainstream, second-run movies. Bruno had other establishments for porn.

The films shown at the Bambi Kino may have been respectable, but the living quarters assigned to the Beatles sure as hell were not. The two rooms were sparse and filthy. The larger room was furnished with two old "field" beds and a small couch. John and Stu, the elders of the group, took the beds, leaving the couch for seventeen-year-old George. The other room's bunk beds were claimed by Paul and Pete. These grand accommodations offered no bedding, so they improvised with some old coats and flags found lying around.

Adjacent to the two rooms were two small bathrooms with two toilets, a urinal gully, and sinks that ran only cold water. All the Beatles were smokers, and their chosen occupations are, well, sweaty endeavors when done properly. Yet, the Beatles' sparse accommodations offered neither bath nor shower, only splashes of cold water.

One shudders at the thought of what scents must have wafted out of the backrooms of the Bambi Kino in the heat of the 1960 German summer. Beatle B.O.

As their residency progressed, the neighbors' noise complaints and the remoteness of the Indra from the main Reeperbahn district led Bruno to close the Indra, and the Beatles played their final show there on October 3. The next day, they began playing at Bruno's other establishment, the Kaiserkeller. The Beatles considered this a step up; unlike the Indra, the Kaiserkeller actually had a dance floor. Here, they would continue their long, sweaty musical internship.

Stuart Sutcliffe with his German girlfriend, Astrid Kirchherr, 1961. *Photo: Jurgen Vollmer / Popper-foto / Getty Images*

Although they were now playing a better club and having a better time on stage, the Beatles still lived in deprivation at the Bambi Kino. At least there was now one glimmer of hope for their personal hygiene: Stu had begun seeing a local woman, Astrid Kirchherr. Through this connection, the Beatles could occasionally visit her place, eat real meals, and take hot showers. True luxury.

Things were looking up, but that was not enough for the ambitious Beatles. In late October, they made a fateful decision, the repercussions of which would linger longer than a rim shot on Pete's snare drum and, once again, torpedo their progress as a band.

The Beatles became ambitious to play at the Top Ten Club, a bigger and better club in the heart of the naughty Reeperbahn. However, the club was owned by Peter Eckhorn, one of Bruno's rival proprietors. Being young and still unworldly, the Beatles had not yet formed an appreciation for business or contracts (a lack of engagement on the financial side of their affairs that would famously persist throughout their career as a band). They were not overly concerned about the fact that their defection for a better club would legally constitute a breach of contract.

Although the Beatles' agreement with Bruno extended through the end of 1960, on October 30 they verbally accepted an offer to play at the Top Ten. With the new gig would come new and better accommodations. Upon learning of his abandonment by the Beatles, Bruno terminated their contract on November 1, and the boys took up residence above the Top Ten, having left in such haste that their belongings were still festering in the Bambi Kino's backrooms. Stu, by this time, was already living at Astrid's, and John and George were next in hightailing it out of the Bambi Kino.

Decidedly unhappy over the Beatles' walkout, Bruno decided that revenge was a dish best served with a side of German police. So, he turned the Beatles in to the authorities for a variety of offenses against humanity. First, and easiest, he tipped off authorities that George was underage. At seventeen, he was not permitted to play in the clubs after 10:00 p.m. Yet, he did so every night (under contract to Bruno, of course, but let's not muddy the story with pesky facts). On November 21, George was deported for being underage. He arrived back in Liverpool, dejected and bereft of his bandmates. Having not quite yet embraced the "one for all and all for one" ethos, John and Paul decided that with two other guitarists to stand in for George, the band could soldier on without him for the remainder of the residency.

Paul and Pete finally got around to retrieving their belongings from the Bambi Kino late on the night of November 29. On their way out the door, the pair found a condom in Pete's suitcase. As a parting gesture to Bruno and a burnt offering to the gods of what they hoped was a better future, the two young men tacked the condom to the wall and set it ablaze. As Paul tells it, there was nothing on the concrete wall that could have caught fire, and it quickly burned out, leaving a little black rubber stain on the wall.

On they went. Or so they thought.

Apparently, Bruno's pride was wounded more severely than his cinder block wall, and he made another report to the authorities. This time, he reported the condom-burning stunt as an attempt to burn down his establishment. Bruno should have been so lucky. The dump was probably worth more in ashes than as a second-rate theater and soon-to-be-defunct club. Nevertheless, after Bruno made his wildly inflamed arson allegation, the *polizei* sure enough spotted Pete and Paul walking down the Reeperbahn. They were arrested on the spot and thrown in a German jail for the night.

The next day, the police put Paul and Pete in a car and unceremoniously deposited them at the airport. The two condom-burning Beatles—for the first time in their lives—were put on an airplane. They were deported from Germany and sent back to Liverpool as arsonists.

Stu, mercifully not deported, decided to stay in Hamburg with Astrid. John—the last Beatle standing—left Hamburg on December 7 and made his way back to Liverpool alone. The Beatles' first foray to Hamburg had ended in disaster. For his part, George was relieved at being reunited with his pals within a few weeks of his deportation. George, Paul, Pete, and John were all back in Liverpool before the end of the year. The core of the gang was back together, but their prospects as a band were dim. In fact, the Beatles didn't even have their equipment. Owing to their haste in leaving Hamburg, voluntarily or not, much of their gear was still in Germany. Luckily, through Peter Eckhorn at the Top Ten Club, it was ultimately retrieved and shipped back to Liverpool.

Once again, the Beatles' forward momentum was stopped in its tracks, thanks to a flaming condom on a concrete wall in a filthy backroom of a second-rate theater on a side street in a seedy German city.

POSTSCRIPT

In another startling example of biting the hand that fed them, the Beatles had a falling out with Allan Williams over money, just as they'd had a year prior with Mona Best. It seems they had stopped paying Allan his commissions, using the rationale that he had booked them to play the Indra. In an unsophisticated bit of legal reasoning, they stopped paying him after Bruno moved them to the Kaiserkeller. Despite this stunt, Allan magnanimously offered to let the Beatles play at his soon-to-be-opened establishment, a Liverpool version of the Top Ten Club. Sadly, it burned down before it even opened. Another opportunity lost to another fire, but this one was a much more serious conflagration than the burning condom on the concrete wall of the Bambi Kino. One step forward, six steps back. At least this time they were not arrested for arson.

The Beatles returned to Hamburg and finally played their first gig at the Top Ten Club on March 28, 1961, beginning what would become a ninety-two-night residency there. George was now eighteen, and this time no condoms would be set alight. However, before they could return to Germany, they had to appeal Paul's and Pete's deportation order and get their passport restrictions lifted. The genial Allan Williams, despite having been stiffed by the Beatles a few months earlier, helped them with the process. After submitting statements in which the burning condom was changed to a burning rag, lit merely to shed some light so they could pack, and paying the deportation fines and penalties owed to the German authorities, Paul and Pete had been allowed to return to Hamburg.

The burning condom story is an enigma for any Beatles researcher to navigate sixty years after the fact. Paul and Pete, the most-direct witnesses, have told divergent stories, sometimes even contradicting their own earlier accounts. At various times, their kindling of choice was described as rags or papers. But history suggests that it was, indeed, a condom, and posterity needs to know: Was it new or used? A forensic mystery. To paraphrase Nigel Tufnel, you can't really dust for spunk.

In the Anthology series, Paul abandoned any pretext that the burning object was anything other than a rubber, or what the true purpose of the prank was: "As we were leaving, me and Pete Best, we were packing up and we were the last to leave and he found a condom in his luggage" . . . the burning was "just for a laugh."

Thankfully for posterity, in a 2008 interview, Pete cleared up the enduring mystery of prophylactic provenance when he declared, "Let's get it clear; they weren't used."

Allan Williams in later life, perhaps betraying his feelings about his association with the Beatles, Liverpool, April 9, 2001. *Photo: Allstar Picture Library Ltd. / Alamy*

The grave of Stuart Sutcliffe, Parish Church Cemetery, Liverpool, August 2019. *Photo: Doug Wolfberg*

After writing his memoir, *Allan Williams: The Man Who Gave the Beatles Away*, Allan died in 2016, at the age of eighty-six. In 2000, Bruno Koschmider died at age seventy-six in Hamburg.

Stu Sutcliffe tragically died of a brain hemorrhage on April 10, 1962, at the age of twenty-one. The Beatles learned of his death when Astrid met them at the airport the following day as they were returning for another Hamburg residency. Stu had left the Beatles to pursue life with Astrid as a full-time painter prior to his untimely death. Paul had taken on full-time bass duties, with John and George on guitars.

After their disastrous late 1960 residency in Hamburg, the Beatles would play four more residencies there through the end of 1962—two with Pete, and two with Pete's replacement, Ringo. By their last one in December 1962, they were fed up with the city and returned only in protest, having learned hard lessons about the consequences of breaking contracts and commitments.

It's hard to fathom that a little more than a year from their last gigs in the squalid Hamburg dance halls, the Beatles would appear on *The Ed Sullivan Show*, conquer America, and become the biggest band the world had ever seen.

The Beatles found a way to bounce back. There wasn't a flaming rubber in the world that could stop them.

CHAPTER 3

HOW DO YOU DO IT?
How the Beatles Took a Stand, Turned Down a Number 1, and Killed Tin Pan Alley in the Process

In late 1962, the Beatles were new to the recording studio. They had no hits under their belts and no clout to throw around. At a time when record producers were king—shopping for songs from music-publishing factories, dictating what their artists would record, and typically enriching themselves in the process—the Beatles stood up to their producer and changed music history.

This outsized stand taken by the then-undersized Beatles helped usher in a new era in which power shifted from producers and music publishers to singer-songwriters. This is the story of the song "How Do You Do It?," the man who wrote it, and how the Beatles' rejection of this surefire number 1 hit changed the music industry and helped deal a death blow to the traditional Tin Pan Alley.

At the time the Beatles were working on their first single for Parlophone Records, the "business" end of show business had little room for musicians and recording artists. Musicians were hired hands; they were grateful for recording contracts and obligingly took direction from record producers. Some performers would follow that formula to fame and fortune, but it was the record companies and music publishers that made the real money in the early days of rock and roll.

As record producer George Martin would explain, "It was quite normal in those days to find material for artists by going to Tin Pan Alley." Tin Pan Alley was the name given to an area in a big city during the early twentieth century where the music business flourished and hit songs originated. It might contain record stores, musical instrument shops, and performance venues; most importantly, these areas were home to the nondescript offices of music publishing companies. The name "Tin Pan Alley" came from the constant racket of composers pounding out their songs on tack pianos to pitch to publishers. First applied to describe the music-publishing houses of New York City, the persistent sound of piano hammers on strings was said to simulate a thousand people banging on tin pans. The name has since been used to describe similar areas in other large cities.

London's Tin Pan Alley was centered on Denmark Street, an area of the West End bordered by Charing Cross Road and St. Giles High Street. Lawrence Wright, a music publisher who later founded *Melody Maker* magazine, was the first to set up shop on Denmark Street in 1911. Other music publishers, managers, and promoters would flock to the area over the ensuing decades, including early British rock promoter Larry Parnes, who had booked the Silver Beetles for their first tour of Scotland.

As the music business evolved over the course of the early to mid-twentieth century, a formula—or perhaps more accurately a pecking order—evolved for how music was written, recorded, and sold. This approach dominated the music business from the 1920s through the 1950s.

Producers such as George Martin, who worked for record companies such as Parlophone, would spend much of their professional time shopping for material that the artists contracted to their labels would record. In those days, artists were not signed with the expectation that they would write and record their own music. They were hired because the record company saw them strictly as singers (and sometimes as musicians, although the producers regularly replaced band members with studio talent) who could appeal to the masses, make records, and then go out and sell those records through live performances and radio airplay.

To the public, the star was the singer. "Groups" were not yet a big thing when the Beatles first walked into EMI studios (fun fact: EMI originally stood for Electric and Musical Industries). In fact, after their first rehearsals, George Martin started pondering which of the Beatles he would make the "front man," as in "John Lennon and the Beatles" or "Paul McCartney and the Beatles." After all, the "group" that had inspired their name was Buddy Holly *and the Crickets*. Almost every recording artist up to that time was *Somebody and the Somethings*.

Because the record producer decided what music was recorded, pressed on vinyl, and sold to the public, he held an outsized role in determining what music his contracted artists would record. A producer's boss expected him to sell records—no more, no less.

Perhaps the only players in the mid-twentieth-century music industry with power to rival record producers were music publishers. Music publishers were entrepreneurs who acquired the copyrights to composers' songs and then sold those songs to record companies. In a common Tin Pan Alley practice, producers would often insist, sometimes under a pseudonym, that their names be included in the songwriting credits, which was a lucrative way to supplement their record company salaries. George Martin, it should be noted, never once imposed this shady practice on the Beatles.

Publishers paid composers for their copyrights on the basis of the commercial potential they believed the songs could generate. If they believed a song had hit potential, they might pay more for its copyright; if not, they would pay the composer less. Composers would earn royalties on their compositions, and their income would be based on the commercial activity; that is, recordings, film soundtracks, etc. that the publisher generated from the tunes.

Composers were, for the most part, simply craftsman—nonperforming writers who could pen catchy tunes and help publishers meet the record companies' demand for hits, their stock in trade.

In 1961, Lionel Stitcher was a twenty-one-year-old traveling handbag salesman, a handsome lad who was a ringer for a young Dustin Hoffman. Lionel was neither a singer nor a musician; he didn't even know how to play

Lionel Stitcher, later known as Mitch Murray, with his ukulele and admirers, 1965. *Photo: Bruce Fleming / Getty Images*

an instrument. After trying unsuccessfully to learn how to play guitar, he had slightly better luck with a ukulele, which had fewer strings and was easier to play. He was also attracted to the ukulele by its portability, primarily for the purpose of entertaining women on the beaches in the South of France while on holiday.

Lionel wanted to try his hand at writing songs and decided he needed a "professional" name for his new venture. He christened himself "Mitch Murray."

Just a few months into his attempts at songwriting with his ukulele, Lionel, now Mitch, penned one in May 1962 that he thought had potential. He originally called it "How Do You Do What You Do to Me?" and thought it was just suggestive enough to be "naughty," while still innocent enough to escape a ban by the BBC if it ever became a record.

Barely a week after writing it, Mitch made a demo of his new song at Regent Sounds on Denmark Street, in the heart of Tin Pan Alley. For musicians, he used a London ballroom band called the Dave Clark Five. The session produced an "acetate," a rather fragile pressing that would be used to hawk his composition to the right record company buyer.

It turns out that the Beatles were not the only shrewd young guns making crafty moves in a business where they had yet to earn clout.

Young Mitch was confident he had written a hit. Instead of selling his copyright to the first publisher who bit, he dangled his catchy tune in front of them and then held out until he found a publisher that could land his song a good deal with a good producer and a good recording artist. Only then would he sign away his copyright.

While shopping his tune to publishers, Mitch simultaneously, and somewhat brazenly, put himself directly in front of record company execs—"A&R men" (artists and repertoire), as they were known. After unsuccessfully pitching his tune to Decca Records as a vehicle for its new *Somebody and the Somethings* (Brian Poole and the Tremoloes, the band that history records Decca as having signed instead of the Beatles), Mitch met with Ron Richards at Parlophone on June 7. Ron bit. Mitch's song was on its way.

Ron played the demo for Dick James, the music publisher whose venture with the Beatles would ultimately make them all wealthy, who was described as "enthusiastic" about the song. But Mitch, the shrewd former traveling salesman, refused to sign over the copyright until he knew with more certainty what would become of his tune.

For the next few months, "How Do You Do It?" (as the song was now being called) kicked around EMI studios, its producers sure of its hit potential and eagerly searching for the right band to take it to the top of the charts.

Music publisher Dick James (*left*) with Beatles' manager Brian Epstein (*center*) and Parlophone producer George Martin at EMI Studios, October 2, 1964. *Photo: Bela Zola / Mirrorpix / Getty Images*

On July 27, George Martin decided that his new group, the Beatles, would be given the song to record as their first single. "I was convinced this was a hit song," George declared. "Not a great piece of songwriting, it wasn't the most marvelous song I'd ever heard in my life, but I thought it had that essential element which would have appealed to a lot of people."

George Martin had no reason to believe that his new, ambitious group from the northern provinces would do anything other than what he told them to do. They would, he was sure, manufacture a hit.

Dick James, who was still trying to secure the copyright from Mitch, told the composer the good news: a "group" was going to record his song. As Mitch recalled, his first reaction was "What do you mean *group?* I didn't know what a 'group' was."

Not even four months after he strummed his ukulele and wrote his first real song, Mitch Murray's composition was cued up, and the Beatles stood ready to record it as their first single—although they would do so under protest.

As Paul McCartney later recalled, the Beatles were rather unenthusiastic about "How Do You Do It?" They saw their music as having a style and integrity that they did not want to blow with a song they considered to be too white and too light. "We couldn't face the people in Liverpool laughing at us. We cannot be seen with that song!"

But in the summer of 1962, the Beatles had not yet recorded a single, charted a hit, or earned any clout. They realized that they had no choice but to do what their record producer commanded. Between shows at the Cavern and their other northern haunts, they began to rework "How Do You Do It?" more to their liking. They changed the key, worked out vocal harmonies, tweaked some words, and added a guitar solo. They were still uninspired by the song and reluctant to record it, but they knew they had few cards to play. "How Do You Do It?" would be first up at their September 4 recording session, and the ears at EMI were anxious to hear what they had done with it.

John, Paul, George, and their brand-new drummer, Ringo, recorded the song in two takes. John sang lead vocal, George played a well-crafted guitar solo, Paul plucked his bass and sang harmony, Ringo drummed well, and the band rendered the song as a catchy, tight presentation of Mitch's tune, even though the composer would later disapprove of the recording. EMI was confident enough in the Beatles' performance that they ordered the tapes to be mastered. In 1962, a record company would not order mastering unless it was confident the song would be released. John and Paul's composition "Love Me Do" would appear on the B side.

The Beatles' self-confidence exceeded their accomplishments. They realized at the September 4 session that if they were going to make a stand for recording their own tunes and against releasing "How Do You Do It.," the time was now. They had recorded a song they did not believe in; now that it was in the can, they had to do everything they could to prevent it from seeing the light of day as a Beatles' record.

The author on the EMI Studio Two staircase that the Beatles climbed to make their stand against the song they didn't believe in. August 9, 2019. *Photo: Doug Wolfberg*

The Beatles climbed the steps in Studio Two to the control room ("where the grown-ups lived," as Paul described it) and confronted George Martin at the mixing desk. John, as the Beatles' erstwhile leader, was deputized as spokesman: "I think we can do better than this," George Martin later recalled John saying.

For an unknown band that hadn't yet sold a single record to confront its all-powerful producer and make a stand so outrageous as to insist that their own, still-unproven material be issued over a surefire number 1 hit was virtually unprecedented. John Lennon and Paul McCartney were not yet "Lennon and McCartney." They were just two cocky guys in an unknown dance hall band from north of England way.

"I suppose we were quite forceful, really, for people in our position," Paul would later recount. "We knew we had to live or die with our own song." Ringo would later say that their unified stand against "How Do You Do It?" was "one of the magic moments of the Beatles. Thank God we stood up for ourselves. We actually looked him in the eye—which is, you know, very heavy for those days, because he was the producer, and we were the lads."

As Mark Lewisohn would write in his seminal work, *All These Years*:

It was an extraordinary situation. Artists did not stand up to their producers. The Beatles had no rank at all to challenge George Martin's authority, and the risk was huge. Their future hinged on his reaction . . . it could have even spelled the end of doing *this* for a living instead of having "a proper job."

To make the situation even more perilous, George Martin made it clear to the Beatles that the song they had recorded under protest was a sure hit, and he knew a thing or two about hits. George Martin later confessed that the Beatles' stand against "How Do You Do It?" and for their own songs planted in his mind a kernel of respect for "the boys." Their material might not yet have been the strongest, but he admired their confidence and integrity—thoughts he kept to himself at the time.

To the Beatles' immense good fortune, George Martin was an amiable and agreeable man. It was not in his nature to respond to this outsized stand by undersized artists by throwing them out of the studio and releasing "How Do You Do It?" over their protests. George deftly deflected their discontent with a challenge: "If you write something as good as that song, I'll let you record it. Otherwise, that's the song that's going out."

In the days immediately following the September 4 session, "How Do You Do It?" was indeed scrapped, but it would be years before the Beatles would know the real story why. At the time, they believed that their principled stand in favor of their own material had prevailed. In truth, the strong arm of music publishers had once again intervened.

The executives at EMI's publishing company, Ardmore & Beechwood, smelled the most potential in the budding songwriting talents of Lennon and McCartney and wanted the composers' copyrights (although they would ultimately lose them to a better deal from Dick James). They were dissatisfied that "Love Me Do" was slated for the B side of the Beatles' first single. Since Ardmore & Beechwood was an EMI subsidiary, its objection carried weight with George Martin. However, the competing publisher, Dick James, who was still trying to score Mitch's copyright for "How Do You Do It?," was not about to relegate the song to a B side. Ultimately, Mitch still shrewdly held the copyright, and when he nixed the idea of his prized work being stuck on the B side of what he saw as an inferior A side by an unknown "group," that was the end of the ballgame.

Aside from the humiliating request to make his song a B side, Mitch simply did not like what the Beatles had done to it. For one, he did not approve of the use of vocal harmonies, which was a budding trademark of the Beatles, being heavily influenced by the vocals of the Everly Brothers (Mitch would later concede to the wisdom of including the harmonies on his song). For another, Mitch believed that the Beatles' performance was simply unenthusiastic and unworthy of the song's potential. He would later say that he thought the Beatles had deliberately turned in a substandard performance to sabotage "How Do You Do It?" so that their own material would appear more favorable to EMI in comparison.

Ultimately, the Beatles' own composition, "Love Me Do," would be the A side of their first single. "How Do You Do It?," which came precariously close to becoming their first release, would stay on the shelf, its composer clutching his copyright, waiting for another opportunity with another artist.

Ultimately, a powerful producer yielded to the protests of two powerful music publishers, and, somehow, the utterly powerless Beatles had prevailed.

In the meantime, George Martin had challenged the Beatles to write a better song, and he would record it. The ultraconfident Beatles accepted the challenge.

In November 1962, after again objecting to their producer's second attempt to release "How Do You Do It?," John and Paul brought "Please Please Me" to George Martin. After accepting some of his suggested tweaks, most critically a tempo change, George Martin confidently exclaimed over the studio's talk-back mic at the end of the session, "Congratulations, boys; you've just recorded your first number 1!" The man knew hit records when he heard them.

Of course, George Martin's prediction came true, but with an asterisk: "Please Please Me" reached number 1 on the *New Musical Express* and *Melody Maker* charts. However, it reached only number 2 on the *Record Retailer* chart. Since the *Record Retailer* chart ultimately became the UK Singles Chart, "Please Please Me" is not an official UK number 1 (and for that reason was excluded from the 2000 compilation album, *1*).

Liverpool band Gerry and the Pacemakers: Gerry Marsden, Les Chadwick, Les Maguire, and Fred Marsden, 1963. *Photo: Pictorial Press Ltd. / Alamy*

Still convinced he had a hit song on his hands with "How Do You Do It?," George Martin gave it to another Brian Epstein–managed *Somebody and the Somethings* band from Liverpool, Gerry and the Pacemakers. Gerry Marsden and his band, which included his brother on the drums (whom George Martin also replaced with a session drummer in the studio) recorded "How Do You Do It?" in January 1963.

Sure enough, it became number 1 in April. It was perched there for two weeks, until knocked from that position by none other than the Beatles' "From Me to You." In less than a year's time, Mitch Murray had gone from neophyte ukulelist to composer of a number 1 hit. Such was the magic of Tin Pan Alley, where composers wrote songs, publishers bought them, and record companies sold them on plastic.

Mitch Murray went on to have a stellar career, complete with second acts. After teaming up in 1965 with lyricist and producer Peter Callander, he wrote such notable hits as "The Night Chicago Died," recorded by Paper Lace, and "Billy Don't Be a Hero," a 1970s number 1 for Bo Donaldson and the Heywoods (and a childhood favorite of this author). He received two Ivor Novello awards (a British version of the Grammys) and was made a Commander of the British Empire in 2019. Mitch also enjoyed a successful career as a humorist and lecturer, and he lives today on the Isle of Man.

The Beatles' version of "How Do You Do It?" was released in 1995 on *Anthology 1*. Although Mitch Murray made no secret of the fact that he was no fan of the Beatles' arrangement of his first hit song and vetoed its consideration for the B side of their first single, as he put it in 2017, he was "very grateful for the royalties" that came his way from the inclusion of "How Do You Do It?" on *Anthology 1*.

In the end, events surrounding Mitch's song benefited just about everyone involved. As Mark Lewisohn put it:

Ultimately everyone won in the "How Do You Do It" situation. The Beatles won, John Lennon and Paul McCartney won, Brian Epstein won, Mitch Murray won, Ardmore & Beechwood won, and George Martin, though he didn't know it, also won. Dick James was the only party to miss out, but there seemed no reason to lose sleep over it, and in time he'd both sign up Murray's song *and* land a bigger prize.

But there was one loser in the Beatles' stand to record their own music: Tin Pan Alley.

The early 1960s marked the emergence of the singer-songwriter and the decline of the composer-publisher-producer money machine that supplied the public with music for nearly a half century. The Beatles were not the first performers to write and record their own songs; Hank Williams, Ray Charles, Jerry Lee Lewis, Buddy Holly, Bob Dylan, and others had done it before them. But it was not until the arrival of the Beatles in the early 1960s that the true balance of power began to shift away from publishers and toward composers who both wrote and recorded their own songs.

And, thanks to hard lessons learned by Lennon and McCartney and other early singer-songwriters, popular music composers would come to appreciate the value of holding their copyrights instead of selling them to publishers. As Paul McCartney famously advised Michael Jackson, there was real money in music publishing.

It has been written that the decline and eventual demise of Tin Pan Alley in the 1960s was primarily the Beatles' fault. As one writer put it: "So the Beatles killed Irving Berlin? What a bummer. I love the Beatles, too. This is like being told your favorite uncle ran over your pet dog."

The irony of the Beatles' role in killing Tin Pan Alley was not lost on writer Tim Sommer, when he correctly noted that the Beatles had done so by taking many of the tried-and-true tricks of Tin Pan Alley composers and adopting them as their own. "Perhaps the single most seismic act of the Beatles was introducing the relatively rigid . . . Tin Pan Alley form of songwriting [the verse/chorus/verse/chorus/bridge/chorus format] to British electric beat groups."

As outstanding composers, musicians, and performers, the Beatles had the good fortune of possessing all the skills necessary to realign the paradigm of the music business. With so much talent in a self-contained unit, the Beatles quite simply had no need to rely on outside composers, and that self-reliance changed the industry forever.

POSTSCRIPT

Further delicious irony is found in the fact that Lennon and McCartney became something of their own Tin Pan Alley after killing the traditional one. In the prolific process of composing material for the Beatles, they became a solid song factory for other artists. Although many artists would cover the Beatles' songs, some also benefited from Lennon and McCartney compositions that were *not* recorded or released by the Beatles. Most notably, the Brian Epstein / NEMS–managed Billy J. Kramer & the Dakotas scored hits with multiple Lennon and McCartney compositions, including both sides of their first single, "Do You Want to Know a Secret" and "I'll Be on My Way," "Bad to Me," "I'm in Love," and "I'll Keep You Satisfied," among others.

Lennon and McCartney also composed songs that became hits for Peter & Gordon and Cilla Black, and later for artists such as Mary Hopkin and Badfinger. Although in some cases their compositions were written specifically for other artists, John and Paul primarily gave away songs they thought were inferior or more stylistically suited to other artists.

Denmark Street, the heart of London's Tin Pan Alley, has been undergoing renovation and redevelopment since the first few years of the 2000s, although not without controversy over the loss of its landmarks critical to British musical history. The area is still home to music stores, studios, and small performance venues, but its status as the center of Britain's music-publishing empire is long gone.

Future generations will not remember the music publishers who sold hit songs to record companies. They will not be able to summon from memory the names of the composers who wrote but didn't perform them. They will remember the artists who sang and performed them, and the Beatles did more than any other act in musical history to forever shift that balance of power in the music business.

CHAPTER 4

ONE SONG, THREE DRUMMERS
The Tortured Tale of Recording the Beatles' First Single

In the spring of 1962, the scrappy, studio-untested Beatles had in their hands a hard-won contract with Parlophone Records. Not yet completely sold on the new act, producer George Martin summoned John, Paul, George, and Pete to EMI Studios on June 6 for an "artist test." They nervously recorded a mixed-tempo, lackluster version of their original composition "Love Me Do."

A recording of the Beatles' first EMI track was in the can, but the long and winding road of their first single was just beginning. This is the story of how it took three different drummers three tries to complete one song, and how the drummer who played on the world's best-known version became a footnote to history, whereas the one who played on the discarded version became a legend.

It was New Year's Day of 1962, at the time just another workday, not yet a bank holiday in England. The Beatles made their first "real" trip to a recording studio, save for some poor-quality demos and a couple of tracks in Germany. John, Paul, George, and Pete were auditioning for Decca Records in between residencies at clubs in Hamburg, Germany.

In a marathon, fifteen-song session, the Beatles recorded mostly covers of songs written by other composers. In fact, only three of the songs they recorded that day were original Lennon and McCartney compositions. "Love Me Do" was not yet in their repertoire. Interestingly, none of the three originals recorded at the Decca audition ended up on any of the Beatles' subsequent studio albums. Apparently, John and Paul themselves must not have thought this material was up to snuff.

After an agonizing wait of about a month with no word from Decca, the label summarily rejected the Beatles. John, Paul, George, Pete, and manager Brian Epstein were crushed.

Although the Beatles didn't know it at the time, a series of events were coalescing behind the scenes that would lead to a new recording opportunity with Parlophone Records, a subsidiary of British music giant EMI. Chief among these hidden developments was the pressure exerted by Sid Colman, general manager of music publisher Ardmore & Beechwood; like Parlophone, it happened to be an EMI subsidiary. Colman pressured EMI's chairman to sign the Beatles to a recording contract because he believed young Lennon and McCartney had potential as songwriters, and he wanted to secure the value he saw in the copyrights to their compositions.

So, as it came to pass, the legend that the Beatles were "discovered" by George Martin, who keenly sensed the magic in their music and gave them a chance in the recording studio, is not the real story. Actually, the Beatles were more or less foisted upon George Martin by the higher-ups at EMI. In fact, when the Beatles finally came in for their first session, George Martin delegated the production duties to his engineer, Ron Richards. George showed up only later.

The Ardmore & Beechwood pressure came to bear in the spring of 1962. In May, Brian Epstein sent the Beatles a telegram in Hamburg, triumphantly informing them of the EMI recording contract he had secured for them and imploring them to "rehearse new material." John and Paul took this to mean "resume writing songs." It was then that they dusted off their long-abandoned composition "Love Me Do," which a sixteen-year-old Paul had started writing in the living room of his dad's home in 1958.

To prepare for their upcoming EMI session, John and Paul finished "Love Me Do," as well as a few other compositions that ultimately became early Beatles recordings. Although generally not considered to be a standout, breathtaking track today, when compared with their stunning body of work over the course of the 1960s, both the composers and the EMI suits identified "Love Me Do" as the strongest of their originals in the spring of 1962 and thus a candidate to become at least the B side of their first single. But the Beatles were already thinking it had greater potential.

Desperate to become recording artists yet having failed in their opportunity to achieve that dream with Decca, the Beatles traveled from Hamburg to London for their June 6, 1962, date at EMI studios on Abbey Road in the posh St. John's Wood section of the city. Decades after the Beatles earned their place in history, it's difficult to imagine that, at this time, they had failed as recording artists and came armed only with "Love Me Do" as their strongest material.

It was not much on which to pin their hopes.

Those hopes were dealt another blow when it finally came time for John, Paul, George, and Pete to record "Love Me Do." Their nervous, uneven, plodding, and ultimately subpar recording of this track that day shook their producer's confidence and ended in disaster for their drummer.

Back when John and Paul had finished writing "Love Me Do" and started performing it in the clubs, the band had devised a "skip beat" for the middle of the song (this part of a song is often called the "middle eight," referring to an eight-bar section that usually occurs right in the middle of a song). This is a noticeable shift in style and an intentional change of tempo that, apparently, the Beatles had performed confidently enough in the clubs to try in the studio.

But translating the song from the stage to the studio was disastrous. Whether due to nerves, inexperience, or a cosmic shit show of factors, Pete's shift from a straight beat to the skip beat was late. On the recorded version, this delay is palpable, making the skip beat in the middle eight sound like an afterthought. To make matters worse, aside from this *intentional* attempt at a tempo change, there were *unintentional* tempo changes in Pete's drumming, forcing the rest of the band to speed up and slow down to stay with their drummer.

To be fair to Pete, this session took place at a time before recording artists had a "click track" to accompany them; in essence, this is an electronic metronome that keeps all the musicians in time in a studio. But Pete's timekeeping miscues on "Love Me Do" did not help matters, especially when coupled with the recent failure and rejection from their previous studio foray.

After the session, George Martin told John, Paul, George, and Brian that, in future sessions, EMI would use a session drummer in place of Pete. EMI didn't care if Pete remained a member of the Beatles and played at their live gigs, but they did not feel he was a suitable drummer for their studio work.

For a band with big aspirations, but as yet little hope, this indictment of their drummer by their all-important record producer was the final impetus for making a personnel change that had been brewing. As Paul later recounted, a measure of dissatisfaction with Pete had been creeping up on him, John, and George even before they received George Martin's damning verdict on Pete's drumming.

Although the decades have produced differing accounts of why Pete was booted from the Beatles, there can be little doubt that EMI's decision to replace him in the studio with a session drummer sealed his fate. The truth is, however, that there were other factors pushing John, Paul, and George away from Pete. Shy and aloof by nature, Pete often bowed out of the "after hours" festivities and carousing that became a ritual for the other Beatles. Of this was born a social division, a chasm, a frayed bond between Pete and his bandmates. The EMI decision to banish Pete from studio work was all the others needed to finally sever the already threadbare attachment between them. "One for all" became "three vs. Pete."

The Beatles' increasingly busy schedule of bookings in the spring of 1962 meant that it would be some time before they would return to EMI studios. So, for the rest of that momentous summer, the Beatles kept Pete on and continued to play in the clubs. But, with another studio date looming in early September, the time for a change was drawing near. Pete's days as a Beatle were numbered.

"We were cowards," said John Lennon, acknowledging their weak stomach for facing Pete to tell him that his time in the Beatles was over. Brian Epstein was forced to break the bad news in August. Believing he was being called to Brian's office to discuss routine business, Pete was instead given the boot. "They want you out and Ringo in," as Pete remembers Brian's words.

By mid-August 1962, Pete Best's two-year stint as the Beatles drummer was over, and Ringo Starr's had begun, just in time for the Beatles' next recording session at EMI, set for September 4. Since it was obvious to everyone that the June version of "Love Me Do" was not suitable for release, the song was on the docket to record once again at Ringo's first session. The Beatles—now John, Paul, George, and Ringo—trekked to London for their first recording session as the band we know today. George had a black eye, clearly visible in

A forlorn former Beatle: Pete Best at home in 1965 after receiving the Royal Order of the Boot from Brian Epstein.
Photo: Sayle / Mirrorpix / Getty Images

the historic photos of this session, said to have been inflicted by a Cavern fan angered at Pete's dismissal from the band (although the provenance of his shiner is specious at best).

Ringo's drumming on "Love Me Do" on September 4 was a perfectly passable piece of work. It is not a complex song, and with the Beatles having mercifully abandoned the disastrous skip-beat section, its tempo and drum patterns are quite straightforward. But it's what you *don't* hear on the recording that led to the decision to record "Love Me Do" *yet again* with a session drummer just a week later.

Perhaps feeling insecure in his place as the newest Beatle, or perhaps overcompensating to prove that he was no Pete Best, Ringo tried to do more than he was capable of during the September 4 session. Among other things, during rehearsals between takes, Ringo was playing a tambourine *and* maracas while playing his bass drum and high-hat cymbals with his foot pedals, even occasionally using the tambourine and maracas as drumsticks to hit the other drums and cymbals. To the already snakebitten George Martin, fresh off the Pete Best "Love Me Do" debacle, the Beatles drum throne started to look more like a clown car. He must have thought the Beatles were destined *never* to find a drummer up to EMI's standards in the studio.

Even though EMI now had a releasable version of "Love Me Do" on master tape from the September 4 session with Ringo, they would ask the Beatles to make one more attempt at recording it at their next session, scheduled a week later, on September 11. Although it is likely that John, Paul, George, and Brian all knew of EMI's plan to bring in a session drummer for this studio date, nobody told Ringo. The Beatles showed up to find a drum kit—and a drummer—already set up in the cavernous Studio Two, yet Ringo was the only one truly surprised. Seated at the kit was thirty-two-year-old Scottish session drummer Andy White, ready to record with these lads who were much younger than he.

Andy White was a well-known, experienced drummer in England, having played for years with a popular fifteen-piece swing band. But the man also had rock cred: he'd played on the important 1960 album *The Sound of Fury* by Billy Fury and toured on bills with Bill Haley, the Platters, and Little Richard. By 1962, Andy had become an established session drummer, having worked on several occasions with EMI engineer Ron Richards. It was Richards who reached out to Andy to book him for the September 11 session. It speaks to the continued place of the Beatles at the low end of the Parlophone artist food chain that George Martin delegated the session drummer outsourcing to his subordinate.

The primary purpose of the September 11 session was to complete both the A and B sides of the Beatles' first single. George Martin was sure that the A side would be a cover of a Mitch Murray song called "How Do

British session drummer Andy White, circa 1985. *Photo: Courtesy Tom Frangione*

You Do It?" (see chapter 3). The working assumption was that "Love Me Do" would be the B side.

After completing a satisfactory version of "How Do You Do It?," the EMI staff suggested they make another attempt at recording "Love Me Do." This must have devastated Ringo, who thought that the master recorded with him the week prior was suitable. So, with Andy White at the drum kit, the third version of "Love Me Do" was recorded on September 11, 1962. Ringo sulked in the control room at the top of the staircase that famously overlooks Studio Two until Ron Richards told him to go down to the studio and rattle a tambourine during the tracking.

Even though Ringo was relegated to tambourine rattler on the September 11 version of "Love Me Do," he rattled it with gusto. Positioning himself as near as possible to the single overhead microphone that was used to record the entire drum kit, Ringo's tambourine is a dominant feature in the mix.

Parlophone single R 4949, "Love Me Do" on the A side. *Photo: CWB/Alamy*

With this third and final effort at recording "Love Me Do," the convoluted tale of how a seemingly simple song took a torturous three tries in the recording studio—with three different drummers—finally came to an end.

Listeners can readily spot the differences between the three released versions of "Love Me Do," even without sophisticated musical knowledge. The Pete Best version is slower, with the telltale skip beat section in the middle eight. The Ringo version includes no tambourine since he was busy playing the drums. The Andy White version features a tambourine prominently in the mix, competing with, and at times even drowning out, the drumming of the man Ringo viewed as the usurper of his rightful role. Knowing this history and hearing the recorded results, one cannot help but to picture Ringo in the studio that day, forlorn but proudly and defiantly shaking his tambourine as close as possible to Andy's overhead drum mic.

Of the three drummers who played on recordings of "Love Me Do" with the Beatles in 1962, one, Pete Best, became a casualty to history, having been dethroned from the most significant perch in rock history. Another of those drummers, Andy White, became a footnote to that history. The subsequent success of the Beatles, unimaginable as it was in Andy's three hours with them in the studio on that September day in 1962, would make it likely that when his time came, his "Love Me Do" session would probably become the first line in his obituary. Of course, we know what became of the other drummer in this trilogy: Ringo Starr, who played on virtually every track the Beatles recorded from that point forward, became a legend.

POSTSCRIPT

All three versions of "Love Me Do" were ultimately released, although some quite later than others.

The British single, released in England on October 5, 1962, was the version recorded on September 4 with Ringo at the kit (much to Ringo's satisfaction). However, the version recorded with Andy White was placed on the Beatles' first album, released in March 1963. All subsequent UK pressings of the "Love Me Do" single reverted to the Andy White version. Andy also played on the single's B side, "P.S. I Love You," which was also included on the *Please Please Me* album.

Interestingly, George Martin had gone so far as to destroy the master tape of "Love Me Do" made with Ringo on September 4, believing the Andy White version to be superior and wanting to prevent the Ringo version from accidentally being released on subsequent single and album pressings. As a result, when the first Beatles album, *Introducing the Beatles*, was released in the United States in January 1964, the Andy White version was used. When "Love Me Do" was released as a single in the US in April 1964, those American buyers also got the Andy White version.

Because the Ringo version of "Love Me Do" was limited to the initial pressing of the single in England, most singles and albums that went out around the world included the Andy White version of the song. As a result, that became the most popular and well-known version worldwide. The Andy version was also included on *The Beatles 1*—the 2000 compilation of all the Beatles' number 1 singles.

In America, it was not until March 21, 1980, that US listeners got to hear the Ringo version of "Love Me Do," when it was released on a Capitol Records compilation called *Rarities*. Because the master tape had been destroyed, a copy was made from an old mono 45 record. The Ringo version also came out on the collection *Past Masters: Volume One*, released in March 1988. Ringo as a solo artist recorded his own version of "Love Me Do" and released it on his album *Vertical Man* in June 1998.

The Pete Best version recorded in June 1962 finally saw the light of day when it was included, along with several other Pete tracks, on *Anthology 1* in November 1995. Although it was understandably overshadowed by the breathless anticipation of the "new" Beatles track "Free as a Bird," the first in the twenty-five years since their breakup, the release of the Pete Best version of "Love Me Do" provided an important aural record of early Beatles history.

Incidentally, the inclusion of the Pete Best version of "Love Me Do" and other Pete tracks on *Anthology 1* finally netted Pete, who had until then never really profited from his time in the biggest band in history, a handsome payday. Although he has been coy in public about the exact figure, his earnings from the recordings are estimated to be at least in the millions of dollars.

In a near-cosmic coincidence, a *fourth* Beatles drummer also recorded "Love Me Do": Jimmy Nicol played on a 1964 Top Six album called *Beatlemania*, which included the song. Although this version was not recorded with the Beatles, it played a part in Jimmy's temporary gig with the band on its first world tour in 1964 (see chapter 8).

Andy White, *seated*, in the studio with the Smithereens (the late Pat DiNizio is fourth from left) and Sirius XM Beatles Channel host Tom Frangione (*far right*), New Jersey, 2008. *Photo courtesy of Tom Frangione*

After his August 1962 dismissal, the Beatles never again spoke to Pete Best in any meaningful way.

Andy White recorded "Love Me Do" one more time: in 2008, he joined New Jersey legends the Smithereens to record their cover of the tune, which ultimately saw release as a single in 2020 (posthumously honoring both Andy and Smithereens vocalist/guitarist Pat DiNizio) with "P.S. I Love You" on the B side.

Andy White died on November 9, 2015, at the age of eighty-five. Sure enough, the "Love Me Do" session with the Beatles was the first line in his obituary.

CHAPTER 5

BIG B, DROP T
How a Drum Salesman's Sketch Became an Enduring Beatles Brand

In late April 1963, Ringo Starr, eight months into his tenure as the Beatles' drummer, decided to upgrade his kit. Along with manager Brian Epstein, Ringo headed into Drum City in central London and set his eyes on a new Ludwig Black Oyster Pearl set. Brian wanted to feature the band's name on the bass drumhead to compete with the prominent "Ludwig" logo. On the spot, the store's owner sketched out a logo and gave it to his signwriter to paint. The hastily drawn logo became the enduring icon of a multibillion-dollar worldwide brand.

This is the story of Ivor Arbiter and Eddie Stokes, the logo they created, and the surprising sums they earned for their labors.

Before Ringo, most drummers sat in the back and away from the limelight. Now they just sit in the back. They have since found the limelight. Or, in one particular case, the limelight may have found him.

Ringo was one of a small and elite group of drummers who changed perceptions and elevated the role of drummers in popular music. So much so that, in his early days, he prominently featured his own stage name—*Ringo Starr*—on his bass drumhead instead of his band's name. In the spring of 1963, that would all change in a hasty but ultimately iconic way.

Before Ringo joined the Beatles, he played with other Liverpool bands—most prominently, Rory Storm and the Hurricanes. "Rory Storm" was fellow Liverpudlian Alan Caldwell, a flashy, blond-haired front man with a stutter that magically disappeared when he sang. Although Ringo was very much a "band man"—that is, he enjoyed playing with other musicians as part of a cohesive unit—in his pre-Beatles days he was also starting to enjoy attention as a performer in his own right. As he became more popular, he permanently dropped his given name, Richard Starkey, and adopted his

Richard Starkey, with his stage name adorning his bass drum head before he became a Beatle. *Photo: Mirrorpix / Getty Images*

stage name full-time. He even got a featured slot in Hurricane shows—"Starr Time," as it came to be known, in which Ringo took over lead vocal duties on songs such as "Boys" by the Shirelles.

Ringo was becoming a star. He was also developing a reputation as being the best drummer in the emerging Liverpool beat scene.

The bass drumhead is prime real estate in a rock-and-roll band. We recognize it now as a canvas on which a band can present its name or a representation of its image to its fans. But in the jazz, big band, and early rock eras, it also served as a way for the guy in the back to put his name out front. Buddy Rich famously adorned his drums with "BR," and to this day, despite his death in 1987, he is one drummer many Americans can identify by name.

As Ringo's star rose, he began to embellish the front of his bass drumhead with personal touches of his own. At first, perhaps self-conscious about stealing the limelight from his charismatic front man, Ringo used the initials "RS." This, Ringo reasoned, would at least give him plausible deniability that the initials were self-promotional. After all, "RS" also stood for Rory Storm.

But, as time progressed and his personal popularity grew, "RS" evolved into "Ringo Starr" on the billboard that was the front of his kick drum.

Rory Storm and the Hurricanes gained popularity and became a busy, working band, more so even than the Beatles at this point. Among other gigs, they played summer residencies at Butlin's, known as a "holiday camp" throughout the UK. Families would flock to these rural retreats for summer vacations, stay in cabins, and gather for meals and parties with games, contests, swimming, and live entertainment. These gigs and residencies started to take their toll on Ringo's increasingly worn Premier drum kit.

In August 1962, the Beatles invited Ringo to join their band, replacing Pete Best. Ringo agreed, packed his Zodiac Zephyr with his "Ringo Starr" kit, left Butlin's, and headed back to his hometown of Liverpool to meet up with John, Paul, and George. Shortly after joining, Ringo played his first gig with the Beatles. It happened on August 18, 1962, at Hulme Hall in Birkenhead, on the other side of the Mersey River from Liverpool. The following day, the Beatles played the Cavern for the first time with Ringo on the throne. A few days after that, a television crew immortalized another Cavern gig featuring the Beatles.

In all these performances, the name "Ringo Starr" appeared on the front of his road-worn Premier drum kit. As 1962 progressed, perhaps sensing that the Beatles were tighter as a unit than Rory Storm and the Hurricanes, Ringo removed his name from the front of his kick drum. For a few months, the big drumhead was a blank canvas.

As 1963 dawned, Ringo and the others realized that the real estate on his bass drumhead was too valuable from a promotional standpoint to leave blank. But it was the *band* they wanted to promote, not just the drummer. Although John was known as the primary visual artist of the group (having attended art college for a time after high school), it was Paul who sketched

The "bug" logo, in full focus, between Paul (*left*) and John, photographed at the Cavern Club in early 1963. *Photo: Michael Ward / Getty Images*

out some drawings featuring the band's name for Ringo's kit. Because the Beatles' name originated as an homage to Buddy Holly's Crickets, Paul went the bug route in this early design. For a few months in 1963, The Beatles-branded bass drum would be known for its "bug" logo, a script font with two antennae protruding from the "B." And, in the "do it yourself" spirit that still defined the up-and-coming but not-quite-yet-arrived band, the logo was printed on a piece of linen and stretched across the bass drumhead. The color difference between the clean linen and worn drumhead is clearly visible in photos from the brief period in late winter / early spring 1963 in which the bug logo was in service.

One of Brian Epstein's many duties as he guided the Beatles from obscurity to notoriety to worldwide fame was to upgrade the ramshackle and road-worn equipment they had been using in the clubs. They managed to get quite a sound out of their primitive, inexpensive gear, but the next steps that Brian mapped out to raise their profile, including recording and television appearances, required an investment in better equipment.

In April 1963, Brian Epstein accompanied Ringo to Drum City, a shop on Shaftesbury Avenue in London, to replace his Premier kit. Owned by Ivor Arbiter, who also owned Sound City on the southern border of London's Soho district, Drum City was the place to go for a top-of-the-line, professional drum kit. Although Ringo did not yet have brand loyalty to any particular manufacturer, he did have a color in mind—black. However, when Ringo spotted a unique color on one of the swatches in Ivor's shop, he knew he had found what he wanted.

Drum City owner Ivor Arbiter (*left*), in a photo taken in 2010. On the right is a man whose name adorns high–output guitar amps worldwide: Jim Marshall of Marshall Amplification. *Photo: Odile Noël / Alamy*

Black Oyster Pearl was the name of the color the Ludwig company had assigned to its new line of drums, and Ringo immediately fixed on that design for his new kit. Because the color was available only on Ludwig drums, Ringo decided that his new kit would be Ludwig. So, Ringo chose a *color* over a brand. Nevertheless, this moment gave rise to one of the most well-known associations between a musician and a brand in rock history.

Prompted by a little hyperbole from Brian Epstein about how big the Beatles were going to be, Ivor saw the transaction as a promotional opportunity for his line of Ludwig drums. Brian, who was price sensitive, since the Beatles were still a cost center and not yet profitable, started negotiating a deal with Ivor in which Ringo would trade in his Premier kit and pay no more than cost for the new set, known as the Ludwig "Downbeat" model.

Ivor wanted to milk any publicity he could from the up-and-coming Beatles by including the Ludwig logo on Ringo's new bass drumhead. When Brian learned that the Ludwig logo would be featured on Ringo's kit, he was not about to be outdone in the PR department. Brian told Ivor that if the Ludwig name was going to be included, so too should the Beatles', and the band's name should be bigger and more prominently displayed than the manufacturer's. The battle of the branding became a minor point of contention in the deal.

Not wanting to lose the sale and its potential promotional opportunity, Ivor took out a piece of Drum City stationery and drew a big circle. On the spot, with Brian and Ringo in the room, Ivor wrote out in all caps "THE BEATLES"—with an exaggerated B and a "T" that extended below the baseline of the other letters. This uniquely styled letter became known as the "drop T."

The Beatles logo as we know it today was fully formed right there and then, hastily drawn by a drum shop owner salvaging the sale of a single drum kit to a still mostly unknown drummer of a mostly unknown band.

Ivor closed the deal on the new Ludwig kit and gave his logo sketch to a man named Edwin "Eddie" Stokes. Eddie had a regular job at the Leo J. Fisher studio on Bateman Street, but he usually came into Drum City over his lunch hour to work as a signwriter—the guy who painted the bass drumheads for Ivor. Working by hand, Eddie, who only had partial use of one of his arms due to childhood polio, painted the "big B, drop T" Beatles logo on the new bass drumhead, several inches below the prominent "Ludwig" name with its distinctive, cursive "L."

Between the professional-sounding kit, the eye-catching Black Oyster Pearl finish, and the new, visually appealing *painted* logo, Ringo's new Ludwig kit was a far cry from his old kit with its linen bug logo. The Beatles were now a *vision*; they had a look to go with their sound, backed by a new logo that would suit their drummer—and their band—in their rise to worldwide fame.

Apparently Ringo wasn't the first to play his new kit. Ivor Arbiter's son Johnny took a turn before delivery to the Beatles. Note the open shipping cartons on the left. *Photo: Larry Ellis / Express / Getty Images*

After Eddie completed the logo, Drum City delivered the new kit to its customer. Because this particular customer was part of an increasingly busy, traveling band, the delivery took place not in London, but in Birmingham, where Drum City employee Gerry Evans brought the kit to Ringo as the Beatles were preparing for a TV appearance at Alpha TV studios.

The May 12, 1963, show would constitute the world premiere of an iconic new logo. Drum City and Eddie would go on to paint at least three more drumheads for the Beatles in 1963 and 1964.

The Beatles' logo became a world icon. Not bad for a guy who drew it just to sell a drum kit.

POSTSCRIPT

In a Shakespearean twist of tragedy, Rory Storm was found dead at home in 1972, having killed himself at age thirty-four with an accidental medication overdose. His mother was found dead in the same house on the same day. It is suspected that she either had a heart attack or took her own life upon finding her dead son.

Victims of a mysterious twin tragedy: Rory Storm at home in Liverpool with his mother, Violet, 1964. *Photo: Pictorial Press Ltd. / Alamy*

The Beatles went on to worldwide fame and untold riches and became legends in their time. Life turned out more modestly for Ivor Arbiter and Eddie Stokes, the two men who created the iconic logo.

Eddie Stokes was paid a total of £5 for painting the Beatles logo on the bass drumhead of Ringo's first 1963 Ludwig Downbeat kit.

Ringo used a total of seven "big B, drop T" logos over the course of the Beatles career. Eddie Stokes painted heads 1 through 4 in 1963 and 1964, each time receiving only his customary, modest fee from Ivor Arbiter for his work. Drumhead #2, which Eddie painted in early 1964 as the Beatles were preparing for their first visit to America, appeared on the landmark *Ed Sullivan Show* performance of February 9, 1964. This logo was bolder and the letters fatter than on the original 1963 version.

Ringo showing his fondness for Beatles drumhead number 2, painted by Eddie Stokes, 1964. *Photo: Jim Witts / Shutterstock*

Because of its place in history from the *Ed Sullivan* performance, this second Beatles logo drumhead has been a "holy grail" of Beatles memorabilia in auction houses over the years. In November 2015, this author participated in an auction by Julien's Auctions in California, where he witnessed a representative of Indianapolis Colts owner Jim Irsay make the winning bid of $2,050,000 for the Eddie Stokes–painted Beatles drumhead number 2. (In case any reader is wondering, this author's haul from that auction included the platinum record awarded to Ringo in 1977 for *The Beatles at the Hollywood Bowl*, which required a winning bid that was, most assuredly, less than $2 million. By a lot.)

Eddie Stokes died in 1999. Although he may well have lived a fulfilling life, he did not profit in any way from his painting of the Beatles logos, other than the meager compensation that Ivor Arbiter paid him for any typical paint job.

Ivor Arbiter, the man who hastily designed the Beatles logo to close the sale of a drum kit, had a prosperous career in the musical-instrument business, having later formed and sold several companies. He sold equipment to the likes of Jeff Beck and Jimi Hendrix. He also became an importer of Japanese karaoke machines in the late 1980s and 1990s. He ultimately went on to become chair of CBS in the UK.

Despite his other successes, the only compensation Ivor Arbiter ever received from designing the iconic Beatles logo, which branded a worldwide multibillion-dollar enterprise, was that he sold a 1963 Ludwig Downbeat drum kit to Ringo Starr. Ivor died in 2005 at age seventy-six.

According to Drum City employee Gerry Evans, the man who delivered the first Ludwig kit to Ringo in 1963, Ivor Arbiter spent a fair amount of time after the Beatles became famous kicking himself for not registering the logo as a trademark so he could monetize it in the years that followed.

Unbelievably, the Beatles logo was not officially registered as a trademark until the 1990s by the Beatles' company, Apple Corps.

The Beatles logo consists of ten letters. But it is the distinctive "big B" and the instantly recognizable "drop T" that will forever secure its place in the history of music and popular culture. All thanks to a drum salesman and his signwriter.

CHAPTER 6

HUSTLERS OR HEROES?
How the Beatles Penned the First Top 20 Hit for the Rolling Stones

In the waning days of the summer of 1963, a chance encounter between the newly established royalty of British rock and roll and a young, impatient impresario managing an aspiring R&B band would lead to the first Top 20 hit for the latter and generations of controversy about whether this interaction was a mere creative gift—or a premeditated hustle.

This is the story of how the Beatles gave the Rolling Stones "I Wanna Be Your Man," a song with which Jagger & Company made its first splash on the British charts, and how it became a twisted tale of misplaced motivations by the confident songwriting team of Lennon and McCartney.

The young man had grown impatient and exasperated with the unproductive racket emanating from the instruments of the six raw and scruffy musicians who were barely older than he. Needing to clear his head, the nineteen-year-old with outsized aspirations walked outside into London's late-summer afternoon air. The date was September 10, 1963. Famously deciding to turn right instead of left, the budding impresario named Andrew Loog Oldham bumped into John Lennon and Paul McCartney. By then, they were two of the most well-known men in Britain and composers of a number 1 hit, with another knocking on the door. The Rolling Stones needed a song. Their R&B well was running dry. As their manager, Andrew was desperate to find a song for his Stones. He asked the two Beatles to join him at the Stones' rehearsal in progress.

In contrast to Brian Epstein, who was years older than all the Beatles that he managed, Andrew Oldham was younger than all the Stones. He was born in London in 1944 to an Australian mother and American father, who was killed in the war before Andrew made his appearance. A colorful,

Andrew Loog Oldham, *second from left in sunglasses*, with his Rolling Stones. Charlie Watts is on the far left, and keyboardist Ian Stewart is third from the left beside Andrew. Rounding out the group are Brian Jones, Keith Richards, Mick Jagger, and Bill Wyman. *Photo: Dezo Hoffman / Shutterstock*

imaginative, and impatient youth, Andrew was filled with the desire to stand at the epicenter of all that was hip in early 1960s Britain. Possessed of a drive to inject himself into whatever and whoever was "happening" in fashion, music, and popular culture, Andrew found his opening by styling himself as a publicist; that is, someone who could translate words into hype for hipsters hungry to embrace all the bursting color in music and art that was replacing the drab, postwar Britain.

Andrew's first professional foray into Britain's exploding youth culture came in its formative early 1960s Carnaby Street fashion scene. Most notably, he became an assistant to designer Mary Quant, who is widely credited with the culture-defining fashion statement known as the *miniskirt*. Gravitating more toward the music scene, Andrew soon sought out Brian Epstein, the savvy provincial who was remaking himself as an urbane Londoner while guiding the Beatles on their way to what seemed to be inevitable worldwide stardom. That trajectory provided plenty of work for NEMS Enterprises to farm out to eager and articulate young iconoclasts like Andrew.

Andrew was freelancing as a publicist for Brian Epstein and NEMS in early 1963, just as "Please Please Me" and "From Me to You" were making their frontal assault on the British charts and perching the Beatles at the pinnacle of British pop. So Andrew saw firsthand how John and Paul's force both as composers and recording artists was emerging.

In this spring of 1963, Andrew paid a visit to Peter Jones, a writer and journalist who covered show business and, in particular, the burgeoning London pop music scene for the *Record Mirror*. Andrew recalls that he was trying to sell Peter something, "probably an Epstein act, but he wasn't interested. He kept talking about this other group, they were still called the Rollin' Stones then, playing around London." He added that he went to see them on Wednesday, April 23, 1963, at the Station Hotel in Richmond, which housed a club called the Crawdaddy. Andrew recalled walking along the side of the hotel, headed toward the club's back entrance, when he witnessed a couple in the alley having a loud "lovers' tiff." Only after the band took the stage did Andrew realize that the quarreling lover was the singer, and he later came to learn that the woman with him was Chrissie Shrimpton.

Mick Jagger with Chrissie Shrimpton in Soho, London, 1965.
Photo: Daily Mirror / Mirrorpix / Getty Images

When the Stones took to the stage, they perked the ears of the audience, including Andrew and Norman Jopling, another *Record Mirror* writer, who later said, "They came on looking like students, but what amazed me, because I was a huge Bo Diddly fan, was that they could replicate his raw sound." He added that he'd "never seen a British band that came anywhere near that."

That night in Richmond, a part of southwest London, the Rollin' Stones were a six-piece band, comprising the five who would go on to enduring worldwide fame: Mick Jagger, Keith Richards, Charlie Watts, Brian Jones, and Bill Wyman, along with keyboardist Ian Stewart. Impressed as he was with their sound and appearance (aside from that of Ian Stewart, whom we'll come back to later), Andrew did not speak with the Stones that first night. Instead, he went the next day to see Eric Easton, a more established figure in the London music business from whom Andrew was renting an office as a base for his still-inchoate plan of cultural indoctrination.

Andrew explains that although he decided on the night of April 23 that he wanted to manage the Stones, he knew he couldn't book gigs without an agent's license, which he didn't hold. Easton did. Therefore, out of necessity, Andrew brought in Eric as an early partner and persuaded him to see the Stones the next Sunday back at the Crawdaddy. As Easton later recalled, "I went along hoping the evening wasn't being wasted."

To his relief, after waiting outside in the queue with a group of teenagers, Easton found the atmosphere when the Stones played "the most exciting I'd ever experienced in a club or a ballroom. The Stones were producing this fantastic sound, which was obviously exactly right for the kids in the audience." Despite Easton's recollections, Andrew later recalled that the Stones had a number of things "against them," when considered from Easton's point of view. "For a start, as someone like Eric was concerned, Mick Jagger simply couldn't sing. They had also failed a BBC audition, which was very important, because it could stop them getting exposure on the radio."

Despite what might have been misgivings on the part of his more established partner, that Sunday night Andrew introduced himself and Easton to the Stones. They asked guitarist Brian Jones, then the group's leader, to come see them the following day. Unfortunately for the new Oldham-Easton management partnership, the proprietor of the Crawdaddy, Giorgio Gomelsky, had also seen the potential of the Stones and was getting his own hooks into them, having booked them as something of an unofficial manager. He had even produced a short promo film about the Stones as part of his self-appointed management duties.

Crawdaddy Club owner Giorgio Gomelsky (*left*), with Brian Jones in London. *Photo: Jeremy Fletcher / Redferns / Getty Images*

In later describing how the Stones slipped through his hands despite his strong start, Gomelsky reminisced, "If I had drawn up a contract, I suppose I might have become a very rich man, but I never believed in those stupid bits of paper."

Ah, but it is the stupid bits of paper that make the world go 'round. When Gomelsky had to leave Britain for his father's funeral, Andrew saw his opening and made his move, signing the Stones to a three-year deal with Impact Sound, the newly formed Oldham-Easton enterprise, which was to share a 25 percent cut of the Stones' earnings. And thus, Gomelsky's management aspirations for the Stones were nipped for good.

Shortly after signing the Impact deal, Brian Jones inked a recording contract with Decca Records' Dick Rowe, the man who, in 1962, famously turned down the Beatles after their audition with Pete Best behind the kit, a bushel of cover songs, and a few Lennon and McCartney originals. Rowe was now tuned in enough to guitar groups to realize that lightning had actually struck twice; he caught the buzz and signed the Rollin' Stones. Incidentally, and more than a little ironically, it was George Harrison who had magnanimously suggested to Rowe that he check out the Stones as a possible Decca signing. This being the same George Harrison whose own group had been rejected by Rowe scarcely eighteen months earlier.

For the newly christened Rolling Stones, within a span of weeks in the spring of 1963, all the pieces fell into place. At a time when singles ruled the charts, and albums weren't yet the thing, the Stones' first effort for Decca was a cover of the 1961 release "Come On" by Chuck Berry. Released in June 1963, the disc reached a respectable number 21 on the UK charts. A good start, but no blockbuster.

With Andrew Oldham and his ostensible partner Eric Easton now at the helm of the Stones' management, finding a follow-up single for the Stones was imperative. Any wave created by "Come On" had already crested, and still the Stones had nothing suitable to record. The weeks turned into months. Meanwhile, the Beatles were becoming proficient both as recording artists and songwriters, and their efforts were making a noticeable dent in the charts. On the other hand, aside from the recording of a version of the Coasters' "Poison Ivy," which the Stones disliked intensely and persuaded Decca to shelve, they had nothing in the can worthy of release as a single. Although new venues were now open to them, where they could perform as a band with a record in the charts, they didn't have a clear pathway in their progression as recording artists.

The Rolling Stones, it can be said with the benefit of hindsight, were twisting in the wind when Andrew Loog Oldham went outside for a walk and some fresh air on that September 1963 day. The place was Studio 51, also known as Ken Coyler's Jazz Club, in London's Soho district. The Stones were rehearsing some new material in search of their next single, but alas, as Andrew later admitted, "We had absolutely nothing to record."

And here's where the story has diverged over the years, depending on who's told it.

As Andrew tells it, while approaching Leicester Square, "I turned right toward the . . . tube station." As he later recalled, telling numerous interviewers a similar story:

> There, getting out of a cab, slightly tipsy, because they had just received their first Ivor Novello award, were John and Paul. Being slightly tipsy allowed them to be psychic; they said, "What's wrong, Andy?" And I said, "I've got nothing to record."

Andrew goes on to assert that the newly awarded and slightly inebriated John and Paul went with Andrew to Studio 51:

People may or may not remember, one, John and Paul were great hustlers, man, they could sell you anything, they really were good. And two, the 45 rpm was god, and I can't exaggerate how great to see your name on it as the writer. So they were great hustlers. They came down and played "I Wanna Be Your Man" as if it wasn't quite finished. Unbeknownst to us, that had recorded it ten days before, with Ringo Starr.

Mick Jagger is also quoted as saying, "The way John and Paul used to hustle tunes was great."

Actually, the Beatles hadn't recorded anything since July 30, 1963, when they worked at EMI on six songs, none of which was "I Wanna Be Your Man." But we'll come back to that.

There might even be a grain of truth in humor: in his cameo in the 1978 Beatles' send-up *All You Need Is Cash*, in which the real Mick Jagger looked back on the start of the Stones' relationship with the fictional Rutles, Mick said, "He was a real hustler for the songs; he always wanted to sell a song." Mick was speaking of Dirk McQuickly, the fictitious Rutles counterpart to Paul McCartney. But one can't help thinking that the tale was based on the real thing, despite the fact that Mick ends the tale by saying the song was "horrible" and that they never bothered to record it.

Thus, the "hustlers" narrative, according to Andrew and supported by Mick, was that the Beatles were, for some reason, trying to present themselves as songwriters capable of writing a song on the spot in front of the Stones at Studio 51. But the reality, according to "Camp Stones," was that John and Paul had already finished the song, and the Beatles had even recorded it. In other words, according to Andrew, the Beatles were simply hustling the Stones with mock songwriting prowess to sell them on a song.

As Bill Wyman recalled, "They ran through ["I Wanna Be Your Man"] for us, and Paul, being left-handed, amazed me by playing my bass backward. When they left, we started to change things around to suit our sound. Brian tried slide guitar on it, which sounded great. That's how . . . the Stones' second single was born." Wyman, who is widely credited with being a detailed and accurate archivist of the Stones' career, noted that Mick recalled being "surprised that John and Paul would be prepared to give us one of their best numbers."

"Camp Beatles" remembers it differently. In 1980, John recalled, "It was a throwaway. The only two versions of the song were Ringo and the Rolling Stones. That shows how much importance we put on it. We weren't going to give them anything great, right?" Further evidence of the song's

A Beatle and a Stone: John Lennon and Mick Jagger. *Photo: MARKA/Alamy*

status as a "throwaway" is found in the fact that it was conceived and composed as a vocal piece for Ringo, whose limited singing abilities necessitated compositions with melodies encompassing a relatively small range of notes.

Paul McCartney remembered the story by saying that he and John had run into Mick and Keith, not Andrew Oldham, and that they "bummed a lift" off them. As the four of them sat in a cab, the two Stones asked the two Beatles if they had any songs for them. Paul supposedly responded, "How about Ringo's song? You could do it as a single."

You know what they say about the '60s: if you can remember, you weren't there.

Despite the discordant recollections on the subject, it is beyond dispute that the Stones recorded "I Wanna Be Your Man" on October 7, 1963, and it was released as their second single—finally—on November 1, 1963. It entered the British charts and stayed there for sixteen weeks, peaking at number 12. It was the first entry for the Rolling Stones in the Top 20. The song was relegated to a B side in America, backing up their cover of Buddy Holly's "Not Fade Away," which barely cracked the Top 50 in the States.

The Beatles provided a lifeline to the Stones at a time when their fortunes seemed to be flagging as recording artists. But the nagging question remains: Did the Beatles hustle the Stones in the process?

Mick Jagger recording "I Wanna Be Your Man," October 7, 1963, in London. *Photo: Jeff Hochberg / Getty Images*

There can be little doubt that John and Paul recognized the value of compositions beyond their utility for the Beatles themselves. Earlier in 1963, Billy J. Kramer and the Dakotas had charted with the Lennon and McCartney songs "Do You Want to Know a Secret" and "I'll Be on My Way," among several others recorded by Billy and his band. The Beatles' originals also found their way to being recorded by Gerry and the Pacemakers, Tommy Quickly, and the Fourmost, all prior to their encounter with the Stones at Studio 51 in September. The Beatles also indisputably knew that battles were being waged for their publishing rights, pitting Dick James against EMI subsidiary Ardmore & Beechwood. This must have signaled to the young composers that there was value in their work regardless of who recorded it.

Certain aspects of the story of John and Paul giving "I Wanna Be Your Man" to the Rolling Stones can be nailed down with precision. Most importantly, studio logs confirm that the Beatles began recording "I Wanna Be Your Man" only on September 11, 1963, one day *after* the meeting with the Stones at their Studio 51 rehearsal space, and they continued to work on it sporadically during several other sessions in September and October. So, the notion that "I Wanna Be Your Man" was so fully formed on September 10 that the Beatles had already recorded it is simply not true. Of course, this doesn't settle the question of whether the song was completely written on September 10, but we know for certain that it had not yet been recorded by the Beatles.

The Beatles, however, eventually did record "I Wanna Be Your Man," starting studio work on it one day *after* meeting with the Stones in Soho and finishing it the following month. It was released on *With the Beatles* in the UK on November 22, 1963 (a fateful day in America that saw the assassination of President John F. Kennedy), and *Meet the Beatles* in the US in January 1964.

So, the indisputable and documented evidence reveals the following tidy chronology of "I Wanna Be Your Man":

September 10, 1963: John and Paul finish composing the song at Studio 51.

September 11, 12, and 30, and October 3 and 23, 1963: the Beatles record the song.

October 7, 1963: the Stones record their version of the song.

October 29, 1963: the Beatles' recording of the song is mixed at EMI.

November 1, 1963: the Stones' version is released as a single in the UK.

November 22, 1963: the Beatles' version of the song is released in the UK as an album track on *With the Beatles*.

Although Paul's statements over the years suggest that the song was completed before it was offered to the Stones and had already been given to Ringo to sing, John was its primary composer. He said unequivocally that "we finished it off in front of them." Notably, John said this in 1974, decades before Andrew Oldham advanced the hustler narrative.

Less critically for the story, but equally important for the comparative credibility of the storytellers, is that the Beatles did not win an Ivor Novello award until 1964, contrary to the claim, made often by Andrew, that John and Paul were fresh out of the Novello ceremony when he met them. The event they attended on September 10, 1963, was a Variety Club luncheon, where they picked up the award for top vocal group of the year. (For completeness, it should be noted that in his two-volume book *The Lyrics*, published in 2021, Sir Paul recalled that at the time they bumped into the Stones, they were either guitar shopping or visiting the offices of their publisher, Dick James.)

Beyond the forensics of who bumped into whom and when the song was written, two key points of the story seem to defy logic:

One, why would the Beatles need to foster the impression that they'd whipped out the song on the spot to somehow persuade the Stones to bite on it? The utility of the song to the Stones was not dependent on whether John and Paul's songwriting prowess allowed them to write a song in an instant versus laboring over it for weeks prior. That was well beyond the point.

Two, why would it even matter if it was a hustle? The question of when "I Wanna Be Your Man" was written doesn't change the fact that the Stones needed a song, and the Beatles had one to offer. There is no benefit to twisting the tale into a hustle when the simple fact is that John and Paul gracefully offered—and the Stones gratefully accepted—the gift of a single-worthy song at a time when they desperately needed one. Oldham and the Stones telling the story as a Lennon and McCartney hustle seems pointless—and maybe a bit ungrateful.

Whether John and Paul had begun composing "I Wanna Be Your Man" in August or, as most of the evidence strongly suggests, finished it off in Studio 51 on September 10, 1963, the Stones used it to score their first-ever Top 20 hit on the British charts and were well on their way to becoming enduring legends.

All with a little help from their friends.

POSTSCRIPT

We heard there was a group from Liverpool . . . [with] long hair, scruffy clothes . . . [and] a record contract. They had a record in the charts with a bluesy harmonica on it called "Love Me Do." When I heard the combination of all these things, I was almost sick. A little later on . . . we were playing a club in Richmond and . . . there they were, right in front of me . . . John, Paul, George, and Ringo. . . . And they had on these beautiful, long, black leather trench coats. I could really die for one of those, and I thought even if I have to learn to write songs, I'm going to get this.

—Mick Jagger, Rock and Roll Hall of Fame induction speech, January 20, 1988

A telling clue to when "I Wanna Be Your Man" was written is the fact that the Rolling Stones admit that they were bitten by the songwriting bug after meeting with John and Paul at Studio 51. This is certainly supported by the fact that Mick and Keith shortly thereafter began to ramp up their own compositions, ultimately becoming enormously successful songwriters in their own right, not only for the Stones but for numerous other recording artists. Mick confirmed the songwriting influence of John and Paul when he said, "The way they crafted their songs wasn't lost on us." Bill Wyman noted that "Lennon and McCartney start[ed] the fashion of writing original songs for their groups."

Although the Beatles by 1965 had mostly abandoned cover songs in favor of their own prolific compositions, the Stones' self-penned hits began that year with "The Last Time," their third UK number 1, and then the worldwide number 1 "(I Can't Get No) Satisfaction," which sparked a decades-long Jagger-Richards collaboration that endures as one of the most successful songwriting partnerships in history, long surpassing the twelve-year run in which John and Paul actively composed together.

The Stones remained signed to Decca Records until 1970. Dick Rowe had not failed to catch the lightning in a bottle the second time.

Not long after Andrew Oldham and Eric Easton signed on as the Rolling Stones' management team, Andrew set in motion what became one of the sadder postscripts in the Oldham/Stones saga: the exile of keyboardist Ian Stewart. A cofounder of the Stones, Scottish-born Stewart was several years older than the others (born in 1938), although it would later be revealed that bassist Bill Wyman lied to his management and the public, understating his age (born in 1936) by five years to appeal to the band's younger contemporaries.

Stewart was a talented musician and multi-instrumentalist, but his relative age and bulky, lantern-jawed appearance (think Jay Leno) stood, in Andrew's mind, in stark contrast to the other thin, young, and lanky members of the band. Andrew thought that a six-piece band was out of place in the self-contained rock group dynamic that was taking hold in Britain, and, in his words, "Kids can't count to six." At Andrew's urging, Stewart was relegated from band cofounder and performing keyboardist to roadie and behind-the-scenes studio musician.

Stewart went on to play piano and organ on most Stones recordings through the mid-1980s. He loyally loaded vans and set up gear for the Stones over most of the next two decades, while his erstwhile bandmates each went on to fame and fortune (or, in the sad case of Brian Jones, an early death, which seemed to Stewart to be a good reason to stay away

Ian Stewart, perhaps gazing forlornly at what could have been, in 1983.
Photo: Brian Rasic / Getty Images

from the drug-and-alcohol-fueled shenanigans of his bandmates). Despite living what was by all accounts a much-cleaner lifestyle than the rest of the Stones, Stewart died of a heart attack at the age of forty-seven on December 12, 1985. One cannot but help think of the parallels of his life to that of the Beatles' Mal Evans, who also lived a life of quiet, uncomplaining service to his internationally famous counterparts, only to die an ignominious and largely anonymous death at too young an age (see chapter 15).

Despite losing out on management of the Rolling Stones, Giorgio Gomelsky obviously recovered from his dislike of "stupid bits of paper" and became a successful manager and producer, including on his client list the Yardbirds. He eventually immigrated to New York and passed away in 2016 at the age of eighty-one.

Andrew Loog Oldham underwent a legendarily messy parting of the ways with the Stones in 1967 after bringing in Allen Klein, the man who would later notoriously play a role in the dissolution of the Beatles (see chapter 14). Oldham orchestrated the ouster of Eric Easton from the Stones' management team, and Easton eventually immigrated to Florida, where he died in 1995, spurning a deathbed phone call from Andrew as he sought in vain to make amends.

Oldham received his own comeuppance in 1967, when, with the destructive Allen Klein in the background, he was himself forced out of the Stones' management, owing to his increasing drug use and inattentiveness to his marquee client. He went on to form the independent label Immediate Records, from which he managed or produced bands including the Small Faces, John Mayall & the Bluesbreakers, Humble Pie, and other artists of note.

Andrew wrote music biographies, and some would say narcissistic autobiographies—three of them—over the years. Nik Cohn described Andrew, the man who accused the Beatles of hustling the Stones, as himself "the most anarchic and obsessive and imaginative hustler of all." Andrew quoted this passage approvingly in one of his own autobiographies.

The controversial, colorful, and creative Andrew Loog Oldham, who couldn't quite help himself from the needless disparagement of the Lennon and McCartney songwriting team, despite their having pulled his client's chestnuts out of the fire in the summer of 1963, was inducted into the Rock and Roll Hall of Fame in 2014, alongside another groundbreaking British music business manager: Brian Epstein.

One of the more bizarre postscripts involving Andrew, Klein, and the Stones began in 1997, when British band the Verve recorded a composition titled "Bittersweet Symphony." The song, which became a worldwide hit from the album *Urban Hymns*, featured a sample from a recording of an orchestral arrangement of the Stones' hit "The Last Time." The orchestral number was recorded in 1965 by none other than the Andrew Loog Oldham Orchestra. The Verve obtained the rights to use five sampled notes from Decca Records, which owned the master recording, but were later sued by Klein's ABKCO for using larger samples of the orchestral recording than what was originally approved. Klein, in a characteristic bit of self-dealing for which he later became notorious, had acquired the publishing rights to the Stones' catalog as part of Oldham's exit in 1967.

Ironically, the Stones' original recording of "The Last Time" didn't even feature the sampled string passage, but that didn't stop Klein as the publisher from claiming his piece. In even richer irony, the Jagger and

Richards songwriting team had themselves "borrowed" the theme of the 1954 Staple Sisters gospel number "This May Be the Last Time" in their own composition.

The composer of "Bittersweet Symphony," Richard Ashcroft, ended up ceding all royalties from the song's publishing, which amounted to a seven-figure hit. To add insult to the injury Klein had inflicted, Andrew sued for mechanical royalties as the composer of the orchestral version of "The Last Time." Even more deflating to Ashcroft was the fact that when his group's recording of "Bittersweet Symphony" was nominated for a Grammy in 1999, its authorship was credited to Jagger and Richards.

The bittersweet saga over "Bittersweet Symphony" finally came to an end in 2019, when negotiations between Klein's son and Jagger/Richards resulted in the return of songwriting credit and all future royalties to Ashcroft—a "life-affirming" moral victory (Ashcroft's words) if not a financial one, given that the vast majority of revenue generated by the track in the 1990s had already found its way into the pockets of others—namely Jagger, Richards, Klein, and Oldham.

The Rolling Stones, of course, long outlasted the Beatles, by more than fifty years and counting, even touring after the 2021 death of founding drummer Charlie Watts. Although the Beatles are nearly universally acclaimed as the most successful, important, and influential band of all time, their music is most often described as pop, whereas the Rolling Stones wear the crown of "greatest rock-and-roll band of all time" by equally universal acclaim. Their paths intersected in countless ways throughout the 1960s and beyond, but in the beginning, the Rolling Stones received an immeasurable boost from the Beatles at a time when their own success was at a crossroads.

CHAPTER 7
NO FREE LUNCH(BOX)
The Lawyer Who Squandered the Beatles' Merchandising Fortune

As the Beatles became the world's first international rock-and-roll superstars, demand for anything Beatles-related was insatiable. Everything from clothes to clocks, dolls to dishware, and wigs to watches flew off the shelves as fast as the trinket factories could churn them out.

While Brian Epstein was occupied building the Beatles as recording artists, monetizing their live performances, and getting them into the movies, he delegated merchandising to his flamboyant London solicitor. This is the story of the deal he struck, the mind-blowing amount of royalties it cost the Beatles, and the bizarre final act of this theatrical barrister.

Beatlemania began sweeping Britain in 1963, and toward the end of the year it was spreading by leaps and bounds throughout Europe. Brian Epstein, the Beatles' manager, was busy planning for a string of upcoming concert dates in Paris and laying the groundwork for an early 1964 trip to America. Among other balls in the air, Brian was also juggling negotiations for the Beatles to star in their first feature-length film.

On top of his increasingly profitable Beatles business, Brian undertook the management of several up-and-coming Liverpool artists, such as Gerry and the Pacemakers.

According to one of Brian's assistants, Tony Bramwell, requests were pouring into Brian's company, NEMS Enterprises, to license the Beatles' name and likenesses for all manner of products and trinkets. The public was starting to develop an insatiable appetite for everything Beatles, a trend that extended well beyond purchasing their records and attending their concerts. Brian simply did not have the time to deal with the multitude of licensing requests, and rip-off artists filled the void, selling Beatles-branded merchandise *without* asking anyone's permission or paying royalties to the Beatles.

In 1963 and early 1964, the concept of "music merchandising" was not the phenomenon it became in the 1970s with the advent of bands that were also savvy marketers, such as Kiss. Brian saw the Beatles' principal sources of income as records and live concert appearances, and the band was fast becoming Brian's principal source of income. His investment in the boys was finally becoming a profit center rather than a cost center.

Although Brian had authorized the tightly controlled Beatles Fan Club to sell sweaters and badges, he saw merchandising merely as a thin layer of icing on the cake, with the Beatles' recording and touring income being the cake.

David Jacobs, *right*, with legendary pianist and showman Liberace, in London, 1959. *Photo: Bettman / Getty Images*

But the unrelenting deluge of merchandise-licensing requests poured in to NEMS. Brian realized he needed to delegate this aspect of the booming Beatles business and turned to his London solicitor, the flamboyant, high-profile showbiz lawyer David Jacobs. Jacobs's hair was dyed jet black, and he stood a commanding 6 feet, 3 inches. He cut a suave figure in his tailored suits and regularly wore full pancake makeup to court, much to the annoyance of the judges in whose courtrooms he appeared. To David Jacobs, litigation was theater, and he insisted on the starring role.

Brian and David became good friends, although more than twenty years separated them in age. Both were Jewish. Both were dialed in to the entertainment business. And both were closeted gay men in the conservative Great Britain of the 1960s, where homosexual acts were against the law. In fact, evidence suggests that David became a surreptitious tour guide of sorts, introducing Brian to gay people and places in underground London.

In 1963, David Jacobs was an established lawyer in his early fifties. He had assembled a high-profile client base. Most notably, Jacobs represented famed showman Liberace in a notorious 1959 libel case in which a London newspaper columnist had famously called the pianist "a luminous, quivering, fruit-flavored, mincing, ice-covered heap of mother-love."

The unmistakable implication was that Liberace was homosexual and had committed unlawful acts in the UK.

Jacobs masterminded a legal strategy on Liberace's behalf that resulted in a £26,000 judgment for his client. Upon exiting the London court after the verdict, Liberace famously proclaimed, "I'm crying all the way to the bank."

Jacobs filled out his celebrity client roster with the likes of Laurence Olivier, Judy Garland, Zsa Zsa Gabor, and a host of other entertainment notables.

Brian Epstein entrusted the licensing of the Beatles' name and likenesses to Jacobs. Seeing this potential revenue stream as nothing more than a minor sideline—"gravy" money—he gave Jacobs virtually complete authority over the Beatles' merchandising, going so far as to execute a power of attorney (POA) so Jacobs could handle it with nearly complete autonomy.

Jacobs knew little more than Brian Epstein did about music merchandising, which was essentially nothing. He recruited another colorful figure to take the reins of the burgeoning Beatles trinket empire, a man he had met on the cocktail party circuit in London.

Nicky Byrne came from privilege. He had been an amateur race car driver who also worked in his wife's clothing boutique, dabbled in theater production, and managed the Condor Club, a well-known party spot in Soho. He was now a thirty-seven-year-old, divorced "man about town."

With Brian Epstein's POA in his pocket, David Jacobs offered Nicky Byrne the opportunity to manage the Beatles' merchandising portfolio. If Epstein and Jacobs both missed the massive lucrative possibilities of Beatles merchandise—and all the evidence suggests they did—Nicky Byrne, most assuredly, did not.

Byrne assembled a partnership with five other men, strangers to Jacobs and Epstein, each of whom chipped in the equivalent of about $1,600 to capitalize their new venture. Nicky christened his new partnership Stramsact and formed an American entity called Seltaeb ("Beatles" spelled backward) to handle merchandising in the US, which he correctly forecast was about to experience a burst of Beatlemania.

On December 4, 1963, Byrne delivered the proposed merchandising contract to Jacobs. The spaces for the relative revenue percentages to be collected by NEMS and Seltaeb were purposefully left blank. When Jacobs called Byrne and asked what percentages he should write into the agreement, Byrne somewhat offhandedly told Jacobs to put 10 percent in for NEMS and 90 percent for Seltaeb. Byrne, no doubt, expected Jacobs either to chuckle or make a counteroffer in response. He did neither.

History does not record whether Nicky Byrne's jaw actually hit the floor.

Nowadays, a typical merchandising contract would net the licensor—the party licensing the rights (in this case, NEMS and the Beatles)—anywhere between 70 and 90 percent of the revenue. The merchandiser receiving the rights—the licensee (in this case, Nicky Byrne and his partners)—would get 30 percent at most, but more likely 10–20 percent.

The signed contract came back from Jacobs with the numbers precisely as Byrne had proposed. The deal was done. NEMS would receive 10 percent, and Byrnes and his partners would get the rest of the income from licensing the Beatles' names and images on everything that moved—plastic guitars, mop-top wigs, lunch boxes, trading cards, record players, Halloween masks—you name it.

Jacobs reportedly told Epstein at the time, "10 percent is better than nothing."

It must be remembered, in fairness to those who made the deal and are no

Woolworth's storefront window stocked with Beatles merchandise. *Photo: David Magnus / Shutterstock*

Ed Sullivan getting into the act in a Beatle wig, 1964. *Photo: CBS / Getty Images*

longer here to defend themselves, that there was no template for rock-and-roll merchandising contracts in 1963. This was literally unchartered territory.

The trinket factories cranked up production. Beatle items flew off the shelves as fast as they could make them. Seltaeb licensed hundreds of items. As the Beatles' first visit to America in February 1964 drew near, Byrne kick-started the promotional bonanza with the help of two New York radio stations, promising free T-shirts for every kid who showed up at the airport to greet them.

Reliance Manufacturing sold over one million Beatles T-shirts in three days. In February 1964, the company president reported that sales of Beatles shirts under his Seltaeb licensing agreement "turned out to be the biggest promotion in our sixty years in business." Remco Toys sold 100,000 Beatle dolls and took orders from retailers for another 500,000. The Lowell Toy company was making 35,000 Beatle wigs a day and was still unable to meet demand.

"Factories were smoking night and day to meet the Beatle demand," the *New York Times* reported in its business news section on February 17, 1964. In this same report, the *Times* noted:

The suddenness of the Beatle merchandising boom can best be illustrated by the rise of Seltaeb: It was formed in New York three weeks ago and has opened, or plans to open, offices in France, South Africa, Australia, and Japan. Seltaeb . . . was licensed by NEMS enterprises, Ltd., of London, which controls all Beatle sales throughout the world.

Another revealing tidbit in the February 17 *Times* piece: "No one involved would say just what cut of the profits the Beatles themselves got, but everyone concerned reports that the Beatles are happy with the boom." What the article missed, apparently, is that ignorance is bliss.

When Nicky Byrne passed along NEMS' first royalty check for $9,700, Epstein innocently asked how much of that amount Byrne was owed by NEMS. When Byrne replied, "Nothing; that's your share, Brian," the enormity of what he had given away sickeningly began to creep into the forefront of Brian Epstein's mind. Leery of the possibility that the Beatles might end his contract if they realized the eye-popping sums of their money he had given away, Epstein never told John, Paul, George, or Ringo the details of his grand miscue.

It did not take long for the Epstein-Byrne honeymoon to end.

Before their relationship went completely off the rails, Epstein and Byrne negotiated a new agreement in late 1964, in which NEMS' royalties went up to 49 percent. However, by then, the biggest bolus of cash from Beatles' merchandise had come and gone, slipping through the fingers of Brian Epstein and the Beatles. Epstein launched his own merchandising company in 1967, but the controversy stirred by John Lennon's "more popular than Jesus" comments in 1966 all but dried up any remaining Beatles merchandising opportunities. The damage had been done. The Beatles had lost out on the truly massive sums that their names and images had generated in 1964.

In December 1964, Brian Epstein and NEMS sued Seltaeb in a New York state court, alleging that Byrne and his partners had failed to pay millions of dollars in merchandise royalties owed to NEMS and the Beatles. Once Epstein fired the litigation starter's pistol, Byrne and Seltaeb countersued NEMS, claiming that Epstein had entered into merchandising side deals, in violation of the exclusive license given to Seltaeb in the 1963 agreement.

In a separate but parallel lawsuit, Byrne's own partners alleged that he was using Seltaeb as his personal piggy bank, siphoning vast sums of cash from the business to underwrite a lavish lifestyle of penthouse apartments, girlfriends, limousines, and helicopters.

In May 1965, the New York court dismissed the NEMS lawsuit, but an appeals court later reinstated it, leading to a settlement in the summer of

1967. Brian Epstein, likely realizing that it was his own poor judgment that lost substantial income for the Beatles, paid the legal costs of the suit out of his own pocket rather than dipping into Beatles funds.

Most financial estimates of the Seltaeb debacle suggest that the Beatles lost over $100,000,000 from the 1963 licensing agreement that David Jacobs signed with Nicky Byrne on behalf of Brian Epstein and NEMS.

To put that number into context, the merchandising profits the Beatles never received would have exceeded the money they earned from *all* of their record sales and *all* of their live concert appearances—not just in 1964, but throughout their career as a band. It would have easily been their most significant source of income.

Brian Epstein was a great promoter. He worked hard to get the Beatles a recording contract, guided their stage act and live concerts, booked them on TV and radio shows, and, it is generally accepted, was more responsible for the Beatles' success than anyone except the Beatles themselves. But what Brian Epstein lacked was the acumen to handle the high-level business

Former Brian Epstein assistant Tony Bramwell (*right*), with the author, at Abbey Road Studios, London, in August 2019. *Photo: Doug Wolfberg*

arrangements that went along with managing the most in-demand pop group in the world. Epstein himself once admitted, "I have no musical knowledge, nor do I know much about show business or the record business."

As former NEMS executive Tony Bramwell put it, Epstein "floundered all the way to the top." "We got screwed for millions," Paul McCartney noted succinctly, adding somewhat bitterly that Epstein "looked to his dad for business advice, and his dad knew how to run a furniture store in Liverpool."

Although the Beatles' financial fortunes ebbed and flowed, the reality is that from 1964 on, they were well off, never again to hold the title of "starving artists." But losing out on more than *a hundred million dollars* is a bitter pill to swallow, even for the Beatles.

POSTSCRIPT

The reinstated *NEMS v. Seltaeb* lawsuit dragged on until 1967. As is common in civil litigation, the parties settled out of court that summer. Brian Epstein must have been relieved to have the matter behind him. But only a few weeks after the settlement was signed, Brian was found dead by his housekeeper at his home in London. On August 27, 1967, at the age of thirty-two, he had overdosed on prescription sleeping pills.

One of the first on the scene of Brian's death was none other than David Jacobs, acting as a "traffic cop" for the chaos that ensued. He officially identified Epstein's body for the coroner.

Although a coroner's inquest ruled that his death was accidental, caused by prescription barbiturates mixed with alcohol, controversy has raged about whether Epstein might have been suicidal. By then, the Beatles had stopped touring, thus removing one of the primary responsibilities of Epstein's Beatles portfolio. And, by 1967, the Beatles must have had an inkling of the massive sums of money they had lost out on due to their manager's inept handling of their merchandising interests in 1963.

Although it's unlikely the Beatles would have completely cut Brian Epstein loose as their manager, evidence suggests that he was worried the band would substantially curtail his place in their lives and business.

Brian Epstein's final visit with his beloved Beatles came four days before his death, on August 23, 1967, when he paid them a visit at EMI Studios during a recording session. The Beatles learned of their manager's death while meditating with the maharishi Mahesh Yogi in Wales and made a hasty return to London in stunned sorrow.

By far, the most lurid postscript of the Beatles' merchandising mishaps involves the man who, history shows, bears the brunt of the responsibility for the debacle: celebrity solicitor David Jacobs.

Although he had grossly mishandled the Beatles' merchandising interests, before the full extent of the damage had become known he remained firmly ensconced in the orbit of Brian Epstein and the Beatles.

In 1965, Jacobs lent the newly married Ringo Starr and his wife, Maureen, the use of his lavish home in Hove, East Sussex, to which he had added a wing that resembled a Miami hotel.

In September 1968, Jacobs became involved in a bizarre court case, in which he represented three men who had been accused of crucifying—literally—a Hungarian interior decorator, who had been found half naked and nailed to a cross. Jacobs's representation of the three men raised eyebrows in England; these were not the type of clients he customarily represented. It was reported that Jacobs himself had been questioned by the police in the matter.

Actress Suzanna Leigh, David Jacobs's friend and confidant, in a publicity shot for the film *The Lost Continent*, 1968. *Photo: Mary Evans / Studiocanal Films Ltd. / Alamy*

Shortly after the crucifixion case, Jacobs checked into a clinic for substance abuse and a nervous breakdown. His friends noticed he had been losing weight and seemed to be especially preoccupied. It had also been reported that Jacobs had around this time become entangled with some London mobsters, and he had even requested police protection.

On December 15, 1968, fifty-six-year-old David Jacobs was found hanging in his garage with a rope around his neck. The coroner ruled that the manner of his death was suicide. Not surprisingly, controversy over the demise of this flamboyant showbiz lawyer has persisted over the decades.

Actress Suzanna Leigh, a British beauty who had starred in movies with Elvis, was a longtime friend of Jacobs. Upon returning home from a trip abroad, Leigh read the news of Jacobs's death—a devastating blow. Mere minutes later, the postman slipped her mail through the slot in her door, and she found a postcard from Jacobs, inviting her to lunch the following week. Leigh said, "I was holding the newspaper telling me he was dead in one hand and the postcard inviting me to lunch in the other. [Suicide] didn't seem right."

Nicky Byrne retired to a yacht in the Bahamas. The Beatles' merchandising business had been very, very good to him.

CHAPTER 8

TEN SHOWS AND
A GOLD WATCH
The Eleven-Day Beatle Who
Dissolved into Anonymity

In June 1964, the Beatles were enjoying the dizzying heights of global Beatlemania. They had conquered America in February, but—short of a handful of shows in the US, a few dates in Sweden and France, and shows in a couple of other corners of the UK—they still hadn't undertaken a proper world tour. The day before they were finally set to do so, embarking for Denmark, the Netherlands, Hong Kong, and Australia, Ringo collapsed. He was unable to travel or perform. With tens of thousands of tickets sold, venues and hotels booked, and the world's press primed for a close-up of the most famous band in the world, canceling the tour was unthinkable.

The Beatles needed to find a substitute drummer on hours' notice, and, after a hasty audition, a little-known but versatile musician was fortuitously thrust onto the most coveted throne in popular music history. This is the story of Jimmie Nicol, the ten shows in eleven days he played with the Beatles, and his downfall and disappearance after the high-water mark of his life.

The Beatles looked like dapper members of the English gentry, outfitted in stylish black suits with gray ties, bowler hats, and leather dress gloves. Their conservative costumes were made complete by tucking newspapers under their arms and dangling cane-handled umbrellas, like bankers with motorcars.

The occasion was a photo shoot for the *Saturday Evening Post* at Prospect Studios in London.

Other than a slightly peaked pallor on Ringo's face, the Beatles wore identical somber expressions in the unique photos taken on the morning of

G.O.P. CAMPAIGN PREVIEW
NEW NOVEL ABOUT CHICAGO
BY SAUL BELLOW
SUMMER MADNESS:
THE BEATLES ARE BACK

POST

THE SATURDAY EVENING POST AUGUST 8-AUGUST 15·1964 25¢

THE BEATLES—8 Pages in Color

The Beatles posing at their June 3, 1964, photo shoot, shortly before Ringo's collapse. *Photo: Bill Waterson / Alamy*

June 3, 1964. This would be the final press event—or so they thought—before departing for Denmark and a stretch of concert dates that could properly be called the Beatles' first world tour.

Before the photo session concluded, however, Ringo collapsed, frightfully sinking to his knees, too ill to finish. The drummer was taken to Middlesex University College Hospital and diagnosed with tonsillitis and pharyngitis.

In an era when tonsillectomies and inpatient hospital stays were the standard of care for what is now a routine condition managed on an outpatient basis and without surgery, doctors admitted Ringo and forbade him to travel.

Grounding a Beatle in June 1964 was like holding back the ocean with a broom. The sweeping, unrelenting tide of Beatlemania and the demands for personal appearances and concerts throughout the world left zero time for debilitating illness and convalescence. Promoters had booked concert venues, blocked hotel suites, and sold tickets in numbers never seen before. In a time before illness and other *force majeure* clauses were standard in entertainment contracts, the Beatles and their manager faced a potential financial calamity if tour dates were canceled. The kickoff show was slated for the next evening in Copenhagen, and the Beatles would be flying out of London in just over twenty-four hours.

Brian Epstein was desperate. Always the actor, Brian decreed that the show must, indeed, go on.

Although Paul and John readily acceded to Brian's plan for recruiting a substitute drummer and starting the tour as scheduled, George was reluctant. At only twenty-one, George was possessed of a wisdom and loyalty beyond his years and resented the way Brian was forcing the Beatles to abandon Ringo when he was ill. It was George who had argued most strenuously to add Ringo to the band in 1962, and the two had grown to be close and loyal friends, a bond that transcended the later disintegration of the band and lasted to the moment of George's death in 2001.

George Martin later recalled George saying, "If Ringo's not part of the group, it's not the Beatles. I don't see why we should do it, and I'm not going to."

The producer-manager tandem, George Martin and Brian Epstein, persuaded George that he would be letting everybody down by backing out of their tour dates at the last minute. George reluctantly accepted their entreaties, and the mad scramble began to backfill the most famous throne in music for however long it would prove to be necessary. At first, they forecasted it would be only four days.

It didn't take long for George (Martin) and Brian to identify a possible understudy percussionist; indeed, there was no time for a protracted search. If Pete Best was considered at all, it was fleeting, and the drummer who had been jettisoned by the group not even two years prior was almost as quickly discounted from contention. The parting had been too abrupt and awkward, and the monumental success the Beatles had achieved after Pete's sacking was just salt on the wound. Intuitively, Brian also did not want to send the message that the group had somehow changed its mind about Ringo and was returning to Pete. John said that a temporary return would not look good for Pete, either, as he tried to make his way with his own post-Beatles band.

The Beatles' handlers would not look backward to fill Ringo's spot. They had to look elsewhere. And they had to look fast. Brian Epstein deputized Neil Aspinall to scour the clubs and try to scare up a drummer, while Brian himself took to the phones. They did not want someone who was famous in his own right or who would claim an undue share of the limelight. They needed someone musically competent and relatively unknown. And with no time to outfit the replacement for a stage wardrobe, the sub had to fit into the jockey-sized Ringo's undersized clothes—literally.

Jimmie Nicol, born in a London town on the south bank of the Thames as James George Nicol in 1939 (thus making him older than any of the Beatles), was a known quantity to at least one Beatle and one key member of the band's inner circle. Jimmie had risen to the rank of a notable studio drummer on the London scene, having recorded for a few UK record labels. Most importantly for the fortuitous call he was about to receive, Jimmie had played on a Top Six record of Beatles covers; six tracks designed either to confuse purchasers into thinking they were buying the real thing or to provide a less expensive alternative to younger record buyers who couldn't afford the real McCoy. That studio experience, coupled with his own formidable musical abilities, meant that Jimmie was instantly capable of playing a good chunk of the Fab Four repertoire right out of the gate.

Jimmie was talented and versatile, competent in many styles of drumming, including pop, R&B, and jazz. He had recently worked his way up to gigging with Georgie Fame and the Blue Flames, one of the "must see" resident bands at London's Flamingo club, where Paul McCartney had seen him perform. Jimmie's tenure with Georgie Fame would prove to be scarcely longer than his tenure subbing in the Beatles—about three weeks. It was Paul who laid the groundwork with his friend Georgie Fame to make the initial inquiry about Jimmie's availability to tour with the Beatles as Ringo's stand-in.

Jimmie was not the first drummer asked to take this temporary gig of a lifetime; he was the third and had been recommended by the second. Jimmie was hanging out at his flat with his wife, Patricia; young son, Howie; and singer John Hodkinson when George Martin called, asking what he was up to for the next four days. George told a disbelieving Jimmie that Ringo had taken ill and the Beatles needed an understudy to kick off their world tour. He would play the first four days' shows, scheduled to start the next evening in Denmark.

George instructed Jimmie to be at EMI's studios on Abbey Road at 3:00 that afternoon. "The Beatles want to run through some numbers with you."

Jimmie let a few minutes pass to process what he had just been asked—instructed—to do. He turned to Hodkinson and said, "Guess what? The Beatles want me to play drums with them. Ringo is sick and I'm leaving to go on tour with them."

Jimmie later confessed to pondering all the possibilities this unexpected phone call raised while on his way to Abbey Road that auspicious afternoon. He allowed himself to imagine he had a shot at replacing Ringo permanently, just as Ringo replaced Pete in 1962. If that possibility was not in the cards, he still saw this opportunity as a springboard to his own new limitless horizons in the music business.

Although these imaginings were not wholly out of the realm of possibility for someone as talented and experienced as Jimmie—after all, he had paid his dues, and this certainly counted as "a ship coming in"—one cannot help but wonder if his fantasizing planted the seeds of his own discontent with the comparatively ordinary life that would follow his brief stint as a Beatle.

The Beatles on a busy day: a publicity shot following the Jimmie Nicol audition on the afternoon of June 3, 1964, at EMI Studios. It was only earlier that day that Ringo had been taken to the hospital. *Photo: ANL/Shutterstock*

When the afternoon arrived, Jimmie went to Abbey Road with John Hodkinson. Although accounts differ over whether the session was an "audition" or a "rehearsal," the semantics fall by the wayside considering the unflinching gaze of the calendar. The Beatles would leave in about twenty-four hours for Denmark. Whether it was an audition or a rehearsal, the fact remained that Jimmie Nicol was the first and only musician to find his way to Ringo's drum throne on June 3, 1964, and he would be the one whom fate ordained to put the beat in the Beatles for the start of their 1964 world tour.

Although Jimmie had not been playing with Georgie Fame for long and would not be afterward, that didn't stop Georgie from milking any publicity that could be extracted from the fact that he had "lent" his drummer to the Beatles.

A hastily arranged press event allowed still photographers and newsreel cameramen to capture the newly deputized temporary Beatle jamming with John, Paul, and George, who had put on his best game face, despite his deep misgivings about leaving Ringo behind.

The stills and movies show an undeniably skilled drummer who is not yet certain whether the lights shining on him are illuminating the end of a tunnel or an oncoming train. It's hard to fathom how Jimmie must have psychologically processed the virtually instantaneous transition from obscure club musician to Beatle under the world's gaze.

The rehearsal/audition over, Jimmie, Brian, and the Beatles had an awkward conversation about money, with the history books recording a salary offer of £2,500 per show and a £2,500 signing bonus. By the time Jimmie returned to his flat early that evening, a hairdresser had shaped his locks into the distinctive mop top, and a wardrobe assistant had done her best to tailor Ringo's stage clothes to fit the slightly larger Jimmie. Despite her best efforts, Jimmie's legs protruded several inches below the hem of Ringo's trousers.

"In the mirror, I cut a mean figure as the new Beatle," said the new Beatle.

As excited as Jimmie was to buckle in for the forthcoming ride of his lifetime, a sick and dejected Ringo lay in his hospital bed, feeling vulnerable and insecure. Ringo had seen firsthand how the wheel of fate turned out Pete Best and installed him as the Beatles' drummer, right as they sat poised on the cusp of immense fame. He knew all too well that the same wheel could turn him out just as quickly. Even visits by his bandmates before leaving for Denmark did not assuage his anxiety. Ringo later famously said: "I wasn't well, and they'd taken Jimmie Nicol, and I thought they didn't love me anymore. All that stuff went through my head."

Early the next morning, Jimmie found himself in the eye of the hurricane, being chauffeured with John, Paul, and George to Heathrow to board the plane for Denmark. The Beatles—Jimmie included—were hounded for autographs by the flight crew as they boarded the plane early, ahead of the other passengers.

The plane touched down in Copenhagen to a waiting throng of thousands of screaming fans. A similar scene awaited the Fab Four at the Royal Hotel. But they had work to do. Instead of holing up in their rooms, the Beatles proceeded briskly to that evening's concert venue, the Hallen Arena, to rehearse their ten-song set. Notably absent from their usual repertoire was Ringo's live vocal showcase, "I Wanna Be Your Man."

By 6:00 p.m. on June 4, barely twenty-four hours after his phone first rang in London with the world-rocking invitation to play drums with the Beatles, the first of that evening's two shows was set to begin at the 4,000-plus-seat arena.

While Jimmie nursed his nerves in the wings during the performance of opening band the Hitmakers, he summoned his reserves of talent and preparation as a seasoned musician, confident that he would succeed in driving the beat of the world's biggest musical act. But before the Beatles even played a note, their set was further trimmed by one when the Hitmakers rather unusually went back out to play an encore—a nearly universal faux pas for an opening act. Horror of horrors, the band played the Beatles' set closer "Long Tall Sally." In fact, it was this very type of occurrence in their club days—bands on the same bill playing the same material—that led John and Paul to start composing their own songs. They reasoned that performing original tunes was an insurance policy against other bands duplicating their repertoire.

Just the same, Paul gave the opening band an earful after the show; they did not make the same mistake at the evening's second show.

Jimmie Nicol was a seasoned drummer, but no studio or club could have adequately prepared him for an arena full of rabid, screaming fans. Unable to hear Paul's count-in for "I Saw Her Standing There," Jimmie started offbeat, only to be rescued by John, who turned to show Jimmie the rhythm of the 2/4 snare beats with his right hand as he strummed his Rickenbacker.

Despite a style of drumming that was noticeably different from Ringo's, Jimmie performed admirably, with only a few hiccups in tempo and missed cues. Witnesses recall the evening's second show going even better than the first. Jimmie was settling into a groove. He was, at least for now, a Beatle.

The Beatles, with Jimmie Nicol on drums, June 5, 1964, in Amsterdam. *Photo: JJs/Alamy*

Jimmie had the unique perspective of a dual existence during these days. One minute, in his stage clothes and mop-top haircut, and breathing in the rarefied air of John, Paul, and George, he was a Beatle. In the next minute, back at the hotel and in street clothes, he could slip out unmolested, taking in the scene as would any anonymous face in the crowd. This duality allowed Jimmie to experience life as a Beatle, while being able to engage in the local sightseeing and clubbing that his bandmates never could.

After Denmark, the entourage decamped for Amsterdam, where the Beatles appeared on a TV show on June 5, followed by two performances on June 6. A legendary night in the famed red-light district led to this future well-known quote by Jimmie: "I thought I could drink and lay women with the best of them until I caught up with these guys." By all accounts, Jimmie fully immersed himself in the Beatle life with all its available perks.

After completing their duties (and extracurriculars) in Amsterdam, the Beatles flew to Hong Kong via a brief backtrack to London, where Ringo's persistent fever dashed their hopes that he might rejoin them, thus extending Jimmie's original four-day engagement. By now, the looming reality that, for Jimmie, the party could—and would—end on the briefest of notices had decidedly tempered his exhilaration at being a Beatle. The thoughts he entertained about slipping into the Beatles as a permanent replacement for Ringo were evaporating quickly, as talk of Ringo's return date infused their everyday conversations. Jimmie knew his Beatles days were numbered.

While flying from London to Hong Kong, John, Paul, George, and Jimmie discovered a mutual friend on board the plane—Tony Sheridan. The Beatles had worked with Tony in Germany in 1961 and served as his backing band the first time they had ever entered a recording studio, well before their EMI days. Jimmie, by coincidence, had drummed in a band with Tony even earlier, in 1959. The presence of a mutual acquaintance on their long flight cleared the way for a bonding experience for Jimmie and the Beatles.

The Beatles and Jimmie played two shows in Hong Kong on June 9. Next, they made their way to Australia, first stopping in Sydney, although not yet scheduled to perform there. In between their press duties and other local appearances, Jimmie slipped out with Mal Evans for an evening of clubbing, sitting in with the band that supported American singer Frances Faye at the Chequers club. Because of Jimmie's proficiency in a range of styles, from swing to show tunes, the impromptu session went well enough that they talked about Jimmie moving to America and joining Faye's band, although that never came to pass.

While in Sydney, Jimmie also learned that music business wheels were turning back in London to cash in on his new notoriety. Jimmie would be set up to lead a new band—Jimmie Nicol and the Shubdubs. Although his hopes for a permanent spot in the Beatles were dashed, Jimmie's dream of parlaying his temporary Beatle stardom into a higher-profile gig and ultimate success was starting to take shape.

The Beatles left Sydney for Adelaide, where they were scheduled to perform four shows, two each on June 12 and 13. They arrived at an empty airport, only to learn shortly thereafter that seemingly the whole of the city had crammed into the town square, more than 300,000 strong. Even the Beatles had not previously experienced a welcome of this magnitude, and Jimmie found himself nearly overwhelmed. He had truly, if only temporarily, reached the pinnacle of the entertainment business, and indeed of all popular culture.

Ringo, fully healed and showing his now-tonsilless mouth to the press before leaving to rejoin the Beatles in Australia. *Photo: Trinity Mirror / Mirrorpix / Alamy*

Not long after touching down in Adelaide, word reached the Beatles that Ringo, accompanied by Brian Epstein, was making his way to Australia via London to San Francisco. He was expected to rejoin the group at their next stop in Melbourne. Jimmie knew that his shows in Adelaide would be his last as a Beatle. By all accounts, he rocked the house, even requiring Mal Evans to feed him a new set of drumsticks to replace the pair he had pulverized partway through the show. Musicians who knew the Beatles could plainly see that Jimmie hit the drums a lot harder than did Ringo.

Despite knowing that Ringo had arrived in Sydney and was on his way to Melbourne, Jimmie traveled with the Beatles to Melbourne on June 14. It became clear that he was now an "outsider" in their orbit; in fact, when Jimmie had a sidebar conversation with a reporter at the press conference in Melbourne, Brian Epstein gave him a verbal dressing down. It seems Jimmie's separate discussion with the reporter was picked up on one of the press mics and was loud enough to interrupt the "real" Beatles, who were busily answering reporters' questions. Clearly, Jimmie's time was up.

The Beatles in Australia with insider–turned–sudden–outsider Jimmie Nicol, June 1964. *Photo: GAB Archive / Redferns / Getty Images*

The Beatles reunited with Ringo in Melbourne on the fourteenth and made a final appearance with Jimmie *and* Ringo on a rooftop balcony of their hotel. Ringo and Jimmie had exchanged pleasantries, and all appeared happy in the press photos of the event. Early the next morning, while the Beatles slept, Brian Epstein personally escorted Jimmie to the airport. It is likely that Brian's accompaniment of Jimmie was less a gesture of courtesy than it was a means to assure himself that Jimmie was truly out of the picture and on his way back to London. Jimmie's 8:00 a.m. departure meant that there was no final farewell from the Beatles, only a £500 payment and a gold watch bearing the inscription "From the Beatles and Brian Epstein to Jimmie—with appreciation and gratitude." Jimmie gave a final interview at the Essendon Airport as he awaited his flight back to London, even bringing Brian Epstein into the shot at the end to stage a warm goodbye for the camera, belying the fact that the relationship had turned frosty.

Jimmie Nicol auditioned for the Beatles in London on June 3, played ten concerts and one TV show with the band over the next eleven days, and was unceremoniously dropped at an airport early on the morning of June 15. Head spinning.

At the Melbourne airport, with his wages, gold watch, and irreplaceable memories, Jimmie Nicol, eleven-day Beatle, boarded his plane to obscurity.

POSTSCRIPT

While Jimmie sat alone with his thoughts at Essendon Airport in the early morning of June 15, a press photographer captured an incredible image—one of Jimmie, alone, when only three days before he had been at the center of one of the largest and most uproarious welcomes Australia had ever seen. The crowds in Adelaide would stand as the largest that ever welcomed the Beatles anywhere, and Jimmie was in the eye of it all.

Now, he was utterly alone. No bandmates. No press. No fans. Nobody.

To go from the center of a massive frenzy of fevered humanity to utter solitude and disregard in an airport terminal is almost beyond description or imagination. Fortunately for posterity, the image captured that morning tells the story better than words ever could.

Jimmie Nicol, the Beatle outcast alone with his thoughts, Essendon Airport, June 15, 1964.
Photo: AP/Shutterstock

When asked in a later interview how he felt at the time the photograph was taken, Jimmie answered, "Well, if you look at that photograph, that answers your question."

Jimmie returned to England and his new band. A reincarnated version of the Shubdubs, one of his older bands, was now fronted with his name. Although the band crossed paths with the Beatles on a bill in the UK, and they exchanged superficial pleasantries on that night in July, not more than a month after leaving the Beatles in Melbourne, Jimmie and the Beatles never interacted or worked together again.

We don't know if Jimmie was actually paid the £2,500 signing bonus and £2,500 per-show fee promised at his audition, or whether the £500 Brian gave him in Melbourne was a bonus or the entirety of his wages. Either way, by the winter of 1965, Jimmie was out of money and had declared bankruptcy. The plan for him and his record company to cash in on his status as a temporary Beatle simply never materialized, and Jimmie ultimately was divorced and estranged from his son, Howie, who went on to become an award-winning sound engineer.

The Spotnicks, with Jimmie Nicol on drums, 1965. *Photo: GAB Archive / Redferns / Getty Images*

Jimmie later joined a Swedish band, the Spotnicks, and toured the world with them. He abruptly jumped ship in Mexico and remained there for a time, having married a dancer. She became his collaborator in a series of variety shows in Mexico before he left her without a trace. Returning to London, he worked in various bands and then as a construction contractor, resurfacing at a Beatles fan convention in 1984.

Jimmie never published a book and has given only a handful of interviews about his time as a Beatle. He seemed to have a knack for avoiding detection, cementing his consignment to obscurity. Although it was rumored that he died in the late 1980s, subsequent photos of him emerged. Presuming he is still alive, he would be eighty-three at the time of this writing.

In a time when virtually anyone with even the most tenuous Beatle connection would write a book, give interviews, and establish a social media presence to cashier their reflected Beatles glow, Jimmie Nicol stands as one of the few who actually lived the Beatles experience, albeit briefly, but never profited from it. He remains one of the most mysterious and elusive footnotes in Beatles history.

Although Jimmie ostensibly fell off the face of the earth, his influence lives on in Beatles lore in at least one concrete way: Paul McCartney said he took the title of his song "Getting Better" from Jimmie's response when he was asked how he was doing as the Beatles' drummer in the early days of the 1964 world tour. Paul remembered the phrase and immortalized it on *Sgt. Pepper's Lonely Hearts Club Band*.

But over the course of eleven days at the height of Beatlemania in the late spring of 1964, Jimmie Nicol occupied a throne at the center of the musical universe and kept the Beatles' train on the tracks as it embarked on its first world tour.

CHAPTER 9

TWO HURRICANES
How the Beatles Overcame the Twin Storms of Dora and Racial Segregation

As the Beatles' 1964 American tour moved south, they were about to fly into not one but two major storms: Hurricane Dora and racial segregation. Both would come to a head before their September 11 concert took place in Jacksonville, Florida.

This is the story of how the Beatles confronted these two tumultuous events in the summer of '64: one by escaping undetected to a tropical paradise, and the second by using their newfound fame in America as a moral force for good in the flawed nation that embraced them.

More than fifty years before the phrase became part of the popular culture in the United States, the Beatles could truly say that Black lives matter.

Although the Beatles became the first musical artists to play to a desegregated audience at Florida's Gator Bowl, this is only one example in their long history of embracing diversity, inclusion, tolerance, and justice. But before they could play this landmark concert, they had to confront another major storm: a Category 3 hurricane ominously traversing northern Florida.

Over the course of their career, Black music had perhaps the greatest influence on the Beatles of any of their musical forebears. The majority of the artists they most respected and whose music they most enjoyed were Black. White artists, such as Elvis, Buddy Holly, and the Everly Brothers, were formative influences on John, Paul, George, and Ringo, but even those musicians were shaped by Black R&B. It was the music of Little Richard, Fats Domino, Smokey Robinson, Bo Diddley, Arthur Alexander, Ray Charles, and other Black artists that really *moved* the Beatles.

Before and after their February visit to the States, which included the epochal appearance on *The Ed Sullivan Show* and concerts at the Washington Coliseum in Washington, DC, and Carnegie Hall in New York City, the Beatles had recorded a bushel of cover songs by Black artists. These included "Anna" by Arthur Alexander, "Chains" by the Shirelles, "Boys" by the Cookies, "Please Mr. Postman" by the Marvelettes, "Roll Over Beethoven" and "Rock and Roll Music" by Chuck Berry, "You Really Got a Hold on Me" by the Miracles, "Money (That's What I Want)" by Barrett Strong, "Slow Down" by Larry Williams, and "Long Tall Sally" by Little Richard, as well as his medley of "Kansas City / Hey-Hey-Hey-Hey."

The Beatles had also featured dozens of songs by Black artists in their numerous BBC radio appearances between 1962 and 1965, many of which were released in the 1990s–2000s on live compilation albums.

"Black music is my life," said John Lennon succinctly in 1972.

In fact, it has been said that the "British invasion" led by the Beatles in the 1960s was really nothing more than English artists adopting Black music as their own and playing it back for American audiences.

The Beatles in 1964 with Motown artist Mary Wells. *Photo: Trinity Mirror / Mirrorpix / Alamy*

The Beatles' weren't merely color-blind, because that implies they didn't care if the music they loved was made by Black or white artists. More accurately, the Beatles very much embraced, celebrated, recorded, and promoted Black music for what it was: Black music, by Black artists, whom the Beatles respected above all others.

The Beatles' enlightened racial views were going to be put to the test when they decided to tour America for the first time in 1964. Their February visit was spent in something of a bubble: the first Sullivan appearance and the aforementioned Washington, DC, and New York shows simply did not expose them to the full range of mid-1960s American society, despite their brief visit to Miami to play a second Sullivan show broadcast from the Deauville Hotel. They had not yet been let loose on the Bible Belt.

On their 1964 summer tour, however, the cities of Jacksonville, Florida; Montgomery, Alabama; and Charlotte, North Carolina were considered for addition to their itinerary. How would the collision of Beatles enlightenment and midcentury southern segregation play out?

The Beatles' American tour started to come together in January 1964, when the Beatles played an eighteen-day residency in Paris at the Olympia Theatre. While in Paris, Beatles manager Brian Epstein had met with Norman Weiss, a promoter at General Artists Corp (GAC) in New York City. Weiss knew the live-music business well. Although Brian Epstein brought much-needed organization and professionalism to the Beatles' affairs, he had no experience arranging large-scale concert tours, especially outside England, and his Beatles were in hot demand all over the world.

Utter pandemonium surrounded the Beatles' time in Paris. In between their gigs at the Olympia, they had to find time to record songs at EMI's studios in Paris and meet with the producer of their upcoming film, *A Hard Day's Night*. Amid this crushing schedule, Brian met with Weiss to begin planning the 1964 American tour and soon after signed an agreement with GAC to manage the Beatles' American concerts.

Norman Weiss had a keen appreciation for American society in the early 1960s, an understanding that would have been more difficult for Brian Epstein to have fully acquired (although, it must be remembered, as a Jew, Brian was himself a member of a persecuted minority). Among other things, Weiss knew of the deeply rooted, systemic, and officially sanctioned racial segregation practices in the South, legalized by state and local Jim Crow laws.

After Brian engaged GAC to book the shows for the American tour, Weiss and his team began working with local promoters in key cities across

The Beatles in Paris, January 1964, where the groundwork was being laid for their first proper American tour. *Photo: Trinity Mirror / Mirrorpix / Alamy*

the US where the Beatles would stop on this inaugural expedition. GAC had worked out the terms of those contracts in advance with Brian Epstein. On Weiss's recommendation, Brian had included a "rider," or legal stipulation, in the contract that required the promoter to agree to certain conditions. Modern concert riders and their indulgence of lavish rock star requests are the stuff of legends. However, in the early '60s, these performance riders were modest and typically covered logistical items, such as transportation to the venue and equipment needs. Weiss knew Brian's wishes, and Brian knew the hearts of the Beatles. As a result, the Beatles' rider also included these eleven words:

ARTISTS WILL NOT BE REQUIRED TO PERFORM BEFORE A SEGREGATED AUDIENCE.

Although the Jacksonville show promoters ultimately drew the most attention to the groundbreaking desegregation clause, it was a standard part of *all* the Beatles' live concert contracts for each of their American tours in

1964–66. However, it was only in America that Brian Epstein found this clause to be necessary. Systemic and sanctioned racial segregation was not a barrier the Beatles faced in any other countries on their itinerary.

During the winter and spring of 1964, contracts between GAC and the individual promoters for the twenty-four American cities were signed, sealed, and delivered. But in July, the wheels of history turned in a way that effected momentous change in American society—and in Beatles concerts.

After President John Kennedy's assassination in November 1963, President Lyndon Johnson took up the cause of enacting into law the civil rights legislation that the Kennedy administration had promoted. Although JFK enjoyed personal popularity during his presidency, he did not have a sufficiently strong base of support in the South to afford antagonizing conservative Democrats by forcing his civil rights bill through Congress. Nor was Kennedy as skilled as Johnson, a former Senate majority leader, in working the intricate levers of power in the Senate necessary to get such a controversial bill passed.

President Johnson's mastery over Congress, along with his relentless and legendary arm twisting, cajoling, and horse trading, led to passage of the Civil Rights Act of 1964. This landmark new law, among other provisions, banned segregation in public accommodations, such as public buildings and certain businesses. The Gator Bowl was owned by the city of Jacksonville. Accordingly, it was a "public accommodation" under the new federal law, which took effect on July 2, 1964—not quite a hundred years after the end of the American Civil War, and a mere nine weeks before the Beatles' scheduled Jacksonville concert.

Although the law of the land now banned racial segregation in the venues that were booked for the Beatles' 1964 American tour, many cities and states in the South were slow to implement its requirements. Some dragged their feet, while others openly defied federal authority. One notorious institutional segregationist was Alabama's governor, George Wallace, who had vowed "segregation forever." One year prior, he famously stood in the doorway of a building at the University of Alabama in a vain attempt to defy the court-ordered admission of that school's first Black students.

Although shows that were being considered for Charlotte and Montgomery never ended up being booked, it certainly couldn't have helped matters that those cities, like many others in the South in the wake of the Civil Rights Act of 1964, initially refused to comply with the new federal law. John Lennon said at the time, "We never play to segregated audiences, and we aren't going to start now. I'd sooner lose our appearance money." It's

RIDER "A" TO CONTRACT DATED ____April 16, 1964____ BETWEEN NEMS ENTERPRISES

LIMITED (HEREINAFTER REFERRED TO AS "PRODUCER") AND ___W. J. Brennan,___

___WBAM Radio Station_____(HEREINAFTER REFERRED TO AS "PURCHASER").

1. The PURCHASER agrees, at his sole expense, to supply police protection
   to the BEATLES of not less than one hundred uniformed officers, for the
   engagement covered herein, and said policemen will be present at least
   one hour prior to performance and thirty minutes following completion
   of performance.

   If, in PRODUCER's opinion, additional police protection is required,
   PURCHASER agrees to hire such additional police at PURCHASER's sole expense.

2. PURCHASER will furnish at his sole expense the following:

   a. A hi-fidelity sound system with adequate number of speakers,
      four floor-stand Hi-Fi mikes with detachable heads and forty
      feet of cord for each microphone. If sound system and micro-
      phones do not meet with PRODUCER's satisfaction, PRODUCER has
      the right to change or augment the system in order to meet
      PRODUCER's sound requirements. Any costs in relation to such
      changes shall be borne solely by the PURCHASER.

   b. Not less than two Super Trouper follow spotlights with normal
      complement of gelatins and necessary operators.

   c. A first-class sound engineer who will be present for technical
      rehearsals, is required by PRODUCER and this same engineer
      will work the entire performance.

3. PURCHASER will submit to PRODUCER for PRODUCER's approval, a list of
   people PURCHASER wishes to include on his complimentary ticket list;
   in no case will the number of complimentary tickets exceed one hundred.

4. No interviews of the BEATLES or any other artists to appear on the
   show will be scheduled by the PURCHASER without the express written
   consent of the PRODUCER.

5. The PURCHASER will arrange for one general Press Conference the day
   of the engagement. The exact time of that Press Conference to be
   approved by the PRODUCER.

6. Artists will not be required to perform before a segregated audience.

The page from the 1964 American NEMS–GAC tour rider showing the antisegregation clause.
Photo courtesy of Chuck Gunderson, Gunderson Collection / Somefuntonight.com

important to recognize that at the time, John was speaking for a group of four young men, the oldest of whom was twenty-four, who were becoming wealthy but not yet fabulously rich, but who were willing to sacrifice lucrative income to stand for their beliefs.

Before the Beatles could fly into the Jacksonville storm of segregation, however, they had a meteorological storm to contend with, caused by a tropical wave off the coast of Senegal that developed into Hurricane Dora.

The Beatles flew north on September 7 for two shows in Canada. While in Montreal, weather reports made it clear that Hurricane Dora was threatening to impede the Beatles' itinerary in Florida. Originally, they had planned to fly to Jacksonville after their Montreal show, where they would take two much-needed days off, resting on a borrowed yacht before their scheduled September 11 appearance at the Gator Bowl.

On the basis of a suggestion from radio newsman Larry Kane, a Floridian who was traveling with the Beatles to report on the tour, Brian Epstein decided to divert the Beatles and their entourage to Key West, a tropical paradise on the southernmost tip of Florida, to wait out Hurricane Dora. The Beatles' hastily arranged diversion to the Keys wasn't announced, so they enjoyed a couple of days in relative peace and quiet, except for the small crowds of locals and tourists who discovered their presence on the island.

The Beatles in Key West, September 10, 1964. *Photo: Florida State Archives*

Incidentally, on one of the nights in their hotel room in Key West, John and Paul had a deep, alcohol-fueled, heart-to-heart conversation. As Paul wrote in *The Lyrics*, "We got very drunk and cried about how we loved each other." Paul later immortalized this emotional exchange in his 1982 song "Here Today," his self-described "love song to John," written very shortly after his former partner's murder on December 8, 1980.

After leaving Key West, the Beatles' plane arrived in Jacksonville in the early afternoon of September 11. But before they could land, their plane circled the airport in a holding pattern for an even-higher-priority flier: President Johnson had been in Jacksonville surveying the hurricane damage, and "Beatle One" had to wait for Air Force One to clear the airspace. When they did touch down, the outer bands of Dora were still lashing the greater Jacksonville area. George Harrison recalled that "it was windy as hell, and it was dark with heavy black clouds everywhere." The Beatles saw Dora's devastation as they left the airport for their hotel.

Contrary to the myth that has circulated for decades about the Beatles' Gator Bowl appearance, it was not a segregationist stand on the part of the concert promoters that threatened to derail their performance; it was the city of Jacksonville itself. The Jacksonville promoters, three brothers named Bill, Cyril, and Dan Brennan, had a long history of desegregating their concerts and events.

If Brian Epstein and the Beatles' tour managers had not made their artists' stance on desegregation clear, it is likely that city officials would have kept the September 11 Beatles concert segregated, federal law or no federal law, with Black concertgoers relegated to the upper seats of the stadium. However, once it was made clear to the city that the Beatles would not perform to a segregated audience, the city backed down, and the concert on September 11, 1964, was the first desegregated concert to be held at Jacksonville's Gator Bowl.

The Beatles played a windswept, thirty-seven-minute set for about 23,000 fans, no doubt a crowd whose size was diminished by the remnants of Hurricane Dora. Pictures of the Gator Bowl concert clearly show mop tops blowing furiously in the wind.

After finishing their concert, the Beatles did not spend the night in Jacksonville as originally planned. The hotel in which they were booked, Jacksonville's still-segregated Hotel George Washington, apparently had not received President Johnson's memo about banning discrimination in public accommodations. So, the Beatles and their entourage of tour managers and supporting acts, which included Black artists the Exciters and Frogman

The Beatles being whipped by the wind onstage at the Gator Bowl in Jacksonville, September 11, 1964. *Photo: Florida State Archives*

Henry, decided to slip out of Jacksonville in the wee hours of the night and set out for their next engagement in Boston.

The Beatles found the whole business of racial segregation silly—or "daft," to use Paul McCartney's word. As Ringo explained: "We didn't play to *these* people or to *those* people. We just played for *people*." For four young men, all foreigners in America, to take a desegregationist stand in the heart of the Jim Crow South spoke volumes about their fundamental decency. The Beatles unabashedly loved Black music; to their minds, the artists who made that music should rightfully occupy the highest pedestals of all their idols. To see any person of color treated as a second-class citizen simply ran contrary to what was imprinted on their DNA.

The Beatles were not simply groundbreaking musicians. They also played a role in helping to remove America's stain of segregation.

POSTSCRIPT

The Beatles were not finished confronting bigotry in the US when the wheels of their plane lifted off the runway in Jacksonville in the early hours of September 12, 1964.

In March 1966, John Lennon gave an interview with journalist Maureen Cleave of the *London Evening Standard*. In the article that resulted from that fateful interview, John was quoted as saying that the Beatles were "more popular than Jesus." Not a ripple from this remark reverberated anywhere in England. But after the quote was reprinted in the September 1966 edition of the American teen magazine *DATEbook*, intolerant indignation reared its head.

Incredibly, the cover of that month's *DATEbook*, which featured a picture of Paul, also prominently displayed a quote that by all rights should have stirred an even-bigger controversy than John's Jesus remark. Commenting on what he perceived as the sad state of American race relations in the mid-1960s, Paul was quoted on the cover as saying, "It's a lousy country where anyone black is a dirty n*****." Paul's (correct) judgment about the intolerance of much of 1960s America fell by the righteous-indignation wayside when compared with John's "blasphemous" (but also wholly true) statement about the relative popularity of the Beatles and Jesus.

Led by Bible Belt radio DJs, a Beatles boycott began in Birmingham, Alabama, in reaction to John's comment. Mass burnings of Beatles albums, books, and merchandise then spread across the American South.

The Ku Klux Klan, America's white-hooded, racist, terror organization, staged a protest at the Beatles' show in Memphis, the city where, less than two years later, Martin Luther King would be assassinated. A telephone threat had been phoned in prior to the Beatles' performance, warning that one of them would be shot on stage. During the second of their two shows there on August 18, someone threw a firecracker onto the stage, causing each of the others to at once glance at John, sure that someone had taken a shot at the Beatles' resident heretic. The other Beatles were noticeably relieved when John remained standing.

The threats directed toward the Beatles in the South on the 1966 tour, coupled with the road-weariness of the Beatlemania years, led the band to decide to stop touring after their August 29, 1966, concert in San Francisco.

Birmingham DJs Tommy Charles (*left*) and Doug Layton, in a still image publicizing their Beatles boycott movement, 1966. Apparently, people listening on the radio could tell it was Beatles album covers they were tearing up. *Photo: AP/Shutterstock*

They would never again perform a public concert for paid ticket holders. In fact, they would never perform again in public, save for their January 1969 swan song on the roof of the Apple building in London. Incidentally, that show included a "fifth Beatle"—the young Black keyboard phenom Billy Preston, whom they'd known since 1962, when Billy played in Little Richard's band on a bill that also featured the Beatles.

The Beatles' empathy with the American civil rights cause would once again be expressed by the band in 1968, this time in the form of the timeless composition "Blackbird," composed by Paul McCartney. Although the song's origin story has varied over time, Paul is frequently on record saying it was about "Black people's struggle in the southern [United] States—I was using the symbolism of a blackbird."

The Beatles forged a path forward for millions with their music, their lyrics, their humor, and their artistry. Amid all of that, it can never be forgotten that the Beatles as young men also bravely opposed systemic racism and segregation in America, at a time when it was dangerous to lives and careers to do so.

CHAPTER 10

ELEANOR RIGBY
If She's a Creature of Paul's Imagination, Why Is She Buried in a Liverpool Graveyard?

"Eleanor Rigby" was a seminal composition and a landmark moment—both for the Beatles and for popular music. A lament for the lonely, the song's fictitious main character was a creation of Paul's imagination, the first name and surname conjured in separate moments of inspiration by its author.

The fact that Eleanor Rigby was the made-up name of a made-up person made it all the more shocking that the same name turned up on a headstone in a UK cemetery. But it is the particular cemetery in which it was discovered that makes this story truly fantastical.

In 1966, Paul McCartney sat down at the piano in the house that he was living in on Wimpole Street in London. He started "vamping" on an E minor chord, keeping the chord steady while he hummed a melody on top of it. As is typical of Paul's songwriting style, he "blocked out" the words with a nonsensical lyric, nothing more than placeholder syllables to fit with the melody taking shape in his mind. Paul is always casually dismissive of this magical musical process, explaining that he sits down at the piano and merely messes about, seeing where the tune will go and what will become of it.

Paul's modesty is becoming. But this parley with the piano produced a song that can only be described as a work of inspired genius. The finished product, "Eleanor Rigby," stood as a singular departure from the conventions of pop music. Moving away from songs about boy loves girl, girl loves boy, and hand-holding, this masterwork tells a tale of loneliness and death in anonymity, backed with the breathless and funereal tones of a double string quartet.

As a young man, Paul enjoyed the company of old ladies who would tell him charming stories about days gone by. He poignantly recalled one particular woman, a shut-in who lived near his Liverpool council house, for whom he would go food shopping.

While devising the melody atop his E-minor chord, the first fully formed line that he blocked out for the second measure of the lyric was "Picks up the rice in a church where a wedding has been." That, Paul later said, gave the song its central theme and "took the song in the 'lonely people' direction." The song went on to introduce another isolated character, the church vicar, Father McKenzie.

From that point on, the song took shape as a sad, touching lament for the lonely, with John, George, and Ringo all contributing lyrical ideas to support Paul's central theme. One of John's boyhood friends, Pete Shotton (one-time washboard player in the Quarrymen when they were still a "skiffle" group), suggested the idea of bringing the two characters, Eleanor Rigby and Father McKenzie, together at the end of the song. The vehicle that Paul chose for uniting these characters was Eleanor's death—a sad finale for characters whose lives were consigned to loneliness and isolation.

In later interviews, Paul was often asked about the name of the main character in his timeless composition. At first, Paul said, he blocked the syllables with "Miss Daisy Hawkins." He soon abandoned that name, since it didn't sound realistic enough. Paul wanted a name that sounded plausible, the name of someone who, although fictional, could have been real.

The Beatles in 1965 with British actress Eleanor Bron, departing for the Bahamas during the shooting of *Help!* Photo: *Trinity Mirror / Mirrorpix / Alamy*

The grave of Eleanor Rigby, St. Peter's Church, Woolton, Liverpool. *Photo: Doug Wolfberg*

At the time, Paul liked the name Eleanor, which was inspired by the leading lady in their 1965 movie, *Help!* British actress Eleanor Bron played Ahme in the film. Her character, although a member of a fanatical, sacrificial religious cult, becomes enamored with the Beatles and helps them save Ringo, who is unluckily wearing the sacrificial ring, which cannot be removed from his finger.

Paul wanted a surname that sounded as realistic as "Eleanor" for the main character in his new song. While in Bristol, which is about two hours west of London near the Bristol Channel, he spotted the sign for "Rigby & Evens, Wine & Spirit Shippers." Paul said he found Rigby to be a believable surname that caught his eye on his stroll through the Bristol docklands with his girlfriend, Jane Asher.

And thus was born Eleanor Rigby.

"I thought, I swear, that I made up the name Eleanor Rigby," said Paul, describing his dual inspiration for the first and last names of his tragic protagonist.

In the 1980s, a researcher "discovered" a headstone in a graveyard with the name Eleanor Rigby. The location of this cemetery gives this tale a completely cosmic twist.

The Quarrymen performing on the St. Peter's Church grounds on the day John Lennon met Paul McCartney. *Photo: Geoff Rhind via Rod Davis, Scorpion Productions*

Rewind to July 6, 1957. On that summer day, John's band, the Quarrymen, was playing at a festival, known as a village "fete," in Woolton, a Liverpool suburb not far from John's home. The Quarrymen played on a makeshift stage set up adjacent to St. Peter's Church in the village. This was the first time that Paul saw John perform. That afternoon, mutual friend Ivan Vaughan introduced Paul to John in the church rec center, directly across the road. At some point that day, Paul impressed John with his rendition of "Twenty Flight Rock" by Eddie Cochran, a song featured in the film *The Girl Can't Help It*, which both John and Paul loved. John invited Paul to join the Quarrymen, and the two became linked forever through their music.

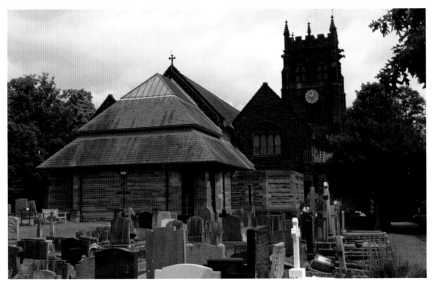

The St. Peter's graveyard, next to the church. *Photo: Doug Wolfberg*

Adjacent to St. Peter's is a graveyard. About 100 yards from the spot where the Quarrymen performed on that fateful day, alongside the church and near the frontage of the road, among the densely packed tombstones arranged in a row, is one with a curious epitaph:

ELEANOR RIGBY, THE BELOVED WIFE OF THOMAS WOODS
. . . DIED 10TH OCT 1939, AGED 44 YEARS.

The grave is located almost at the midpoint between the place where the stage was erected for the village fete and the building across the road where John and Paul were first introduced. Although this headstone is tucked in closely behind another row of grave markers, there can be little doubt that Paul would have walked right by it, not only on July 6, 1957, but on other occasions when Paul and John hung out on the church grounds to lie in the sun.

The real Eleanor Rigby was born in 1895 and was a "scullery maid," a kitchen worker, at Liverpool City Hospital. She married Thomas Woods, so this Eleanor did not exactly die a lonely old woman; however, by all evidence, she had lived a relatively short, childless, and anonymous life when she died at the age of forty-four in 1939, one day short of a year before John Lennon was born.

Although some men of the cloth later claimed to be the inspiration for "Father McKenzie," the truth is that Paul originally named the character "Father McCartney." Not wanting to offend his father, Jim, with the implication that he was a lonely old man, Paul flipped through the phone book to see what came after McCartney and arrived at "McKenzie." Thus arose the other lonely character who came to officiate at Eleanor Rigby's funeral at the song's conclusion.

Paul's quest to conjure a realistic-sounding name hit the mark precisely. So precisely, in fact, that his lonely character shared a name with a real woman who had lived and died decades earlier in his hometown, and whose mortal remains rested just beneath the ground he trod on the day he first met John Lennon.

POSTSCRIPT

When the discovery of Eleanor Rigby's grave was pointed out to Paul, he was as surprised as anyone. Although he was certain beyond any doubt that he had invented the name in two separate moments of inspiration, one from the name of Eleanor Bron and the other from the Rigby & Evens sign, he conceded that the name could have also been planted in his subconscious, given the proximity of the grave of the real Eleanor Rigby to such an important spot in Beatles history. His response: "Did I subconsciously know that name? Why would I go around searching for it? I don't know. I think maybe it's a coincidence."

A coincidence, perhaps, but a coincidence of cosmic proportions.

"Eleanor Rigby" was recorded at EMI Studios on April 28–29, 1966, with additional harmony vocals added on June 6. It was released in August 1966, both as a single (incongruously on the flip side of "Yellow Submarine") and as a track on the landmark *Revolver* album.

The track was a milestone in pop music for several reasons. Its subject matter was a radical departure from the breezy subjects of love, infatuation, dancing, fast cars, and mirth that typified pop songs until then. It began a migration of the Beatles' music from catchy, innocent pop to deeper, more-meaningful subjects, more-advanced melodies, and experimentation with instruments that were generally not used in the pop genre.

The musical score on "Eleanor Rigby" was arranged by producer George Martin, himself an accomplished musician. The entire backing track consisted of a double string quartet comprising eight instruments—violins, violas, and cellos. It was the first Beatles song on which no member of the band played any instruments.

Groundbreaking Beatles recording engineer, the late Geoff Emerick, with the author in 2010, Las Vegas. *Photo: Doug Wolfberg*

Also notable was the revolutionary technique used to record the music. EMI technicians were trained to record classical instruments by placing microphones at a distance from the musicians. This method presumably captured a more ambient feel, with the slight reverberation that came from large rooms such as Studios Two and Three at Abbey Road. However, on this occasion, twenty-one-year-old Geoff Emerick, a recording engineer who worked on *Revolver* and numerous other Beatles records, departed from convention and moved the microphones up close to the string instruments, over some objections by the stuffy session musicians, who found the mic placement unorthodox and constricting. Geoff wanted to achieve for the song's composer a raw, biting quality to the strings, which clearly comes through in their sharp, staccato style.

Along with the instrumentation of the string octet, the voices of Paul, John, and George provide melody and harmony.

The double A-sided "Eleanor Rigby / Yellow Submarine" single soared to number 1 in England and number 11 on the American charts. The song received the 1966 Grammy Award for Best Contemporary Vocal Performance. A gorgeous version was released in 1996 on *Anthology 2*. This version, which includes the backing track only, reveals the beauty and grit of the close mic placement and the double string quartet arrangement.

"Eleanor Rigby" was also one of the recordings that started a fascination among the press and the public with the motivations and deeper meanings behind the Beatles' songs. In virtually every city the Beatles played on their various tours, they were pressured to give obligatory press conferences, and most of the questions asked by reporters in these events were downright banal. They are almost embarrassing to watch now through the lens of twenty-first-century journalism. The Beatles became notorious for turning some reporters' absurd questions into scathingly witty responses.

In one such exchange during an August 24, 1966, press conference in Los Angeles, a reporter asked the following question:

I'd like to direct this question to Messrs. Lennon and McCartney. In a recent article, *Time* magazine put down pop music, and they referred to "Day Tripper" as being about a prostitute, and "Eleanor Rigby" as being about a lesbian. I just wanted to know what your intent was when you wrote it, and what your feeling is about the *Time* magazine criticism of the music that is being written today.

With perfect comic timing, Paul gave this hilariously biting response: "We were just trying to write songs about prostitutes and lesbians, that's all."

A statue to the lonely: an Eleanor Rigby memorial in Liverpool. *Photo: Ed Rooney / Alamy*

Although the verdict of history is that Paul McCartney's inspiration for the title of his groundbreaking song was his fertile imagination, his beautiful and poignant composition about loneliness bestowed immortality upon a previously anonymous Liverpudlian woman twenty-seven years after her death.

CHAPTER 11

IMAGES OF A WOMAN
How Political Upheaval, a Duplicitous Promoter, and a Hotel Lockdown Led to a Singular Work of Beatles Art

Even by the Beatles standards, their 1966 world tour was pure mayhem, and Japan was its first flash point. Amid death threats and a cultural firestorm ignited by their planned concerts at Tokyo's sacred Budokan arena, Japanese authorities confined the Beatles to a hotel suite for the duration of their three-day visit.

The Tokyo shows had been arranged by a noted Japanese promoter. But as the conservative backlash against the Beatles at the Budokan reached a fever pitch, the duplicitous businessman switched sides and joined government officials in protesting the very concerts he had arranged. In between his double-dealing, the promoter visited the Beatles in their hotel, bearing gifts that led to a singular artistic collaboration—the only painting ever created by all four Beatles. This is the story of that painting and the tumultuous Far East tour that produced it.

Over the course of two tempestuous months in the summer of 1966, the Beatles embarked on a world tour that took them to Germany, Asia, and, finally, the United States. Between June 24 in Munich and August 29 in San Francisco, the Beatles would be put through a show business sausage grinder that would bring death threats, typhoons, religious uproar, political protests, and a showdown with a murderous dictator. So physically, emotionally, and spiritually draining was this world tour that it would forever end their live performance career as a band.

The '66 tour began with two dates at the Circus Krone in Munich, followed the next day by two shows in Essen, Germany. The Beatles later remembered these shows as some of their worst performances from a musical standpoint. At that time, audiences still screamed for the Beatles, but the band's frustration grew with each performance as their fear of deteriorating their musical skills and an increasing inability to reproduce complex studio sounds on stage became dominant concerns.

Their last stop in Germany should have been a triumphal return to Hamburg, their first since the two weeks in December 1962, when they played their last residency at the Star-Club. Despite returning with fame and fortune to the city where they had cut their teeth, the Beatles had mixed feelings about coming back to Hamburg. As young men, they had been enthralled by Europe's seediest city, but by 1966 they had been through unimaginable changes, and Hamburg had simply lost its appeal to the Beatles. They'd even received death threats there, an occurrence that was, sadly, becoming more common.

The Beatles' two shows in Hamburg were an obligation, the mere fulfillment of a contract. Although they saw some old friends and visited some old haunts, they would have just as soon skipped Hamburg altogether that summer. George said of this return visit, "A lot of ghosts materialized out of the woodwork—people you didn't necessarily want to see again, who had been your best friend one drunken night back in 1960."

The Beatles touch down in Tokyo, June 30, 1966. *Photo: Keystone-France / Gamma-Rapho / Getty Images*

After a pit stop in London and an unplanned, weather-related diversion in Alaska, the Beatles arrived at Tokyo's Haneda Airport at 3:40 a.m. on June 30. They had planned to catch some shut-eye, see a few local sights, and play their first scheduled show later that evening.

Before the Beatles' arrival, word had filtered down to Japanese law enforcement officials about the German death threats. This set Japanese security personnel even more on edge than they had been. Tokyo was a simmering cauldron of political protest ready to boil over at any minute.

Japan in 1966 was only twenty-one years removed from the crushing, cataclysmic defeat of World War II. In fact, American troops continued to occupy the Japanese mainland until 1952, and Japan had regained its status as a sovereign nation only fourteen years before the Beatles' arrival. The postwar period saw Japan emerge from its destruction, its resurrection culminating in Tokyo's first-ever hosting of the Summer Olympics in 1964.

The Nippon Budokan arena, known as simply the Budokan, was built especially for the Olympic judo competition, the first time the sport had been included in the Olympic Games. The Budokan was built on a site where Japanese soldiers pledged their lives to the emperor before going off to war; it sat between the Yasukuni Shrine, a sacred Japanese war memorial, and the Imperial Palace. Although the Budokan was a competition arena, its vaunted location, coupled with the honor and Shinto spirit intrinsic to judo and the other martial arts, bestowed on the facility a solemn status as a sacred shrine. The hall had hosted other musical shows, but they had been limited to traditional Japanese performers. No Western music had reverberated under the rafters of the Budokan.

Tatsuji Nagashima, or "Tats" as he was known, was in 1966 the forty-year-old son of a Japanese banker. Raised in privilege, he had lived as a child with his family in London and New York, returning to Japan in 1941 as a teenager, just before the declaration of war between Japan and the United States that followed the attack on Pearl Harbor. Children who had lived in the prewar West and returned to Japan were called *kikokushijo* (returnee child), and during the war were often the target of discrimination and harassment for their Western ties. A Japanese artist named Yoko Ono was another notable *kikokushijo*.

Perhaps Tats Nagashima, with his Asian heritage and Western upbringing, was accustomed to living a dual life and bridging both sides of a cultural divide. Whatever the reason, this duality would be on full display in June 1966.

As pop records became available in Japan, and radio stations gave the Beatles substantial airplay, Japan was no longer immune from the worldwide spread of Beatlemania. Tats knew an opportunity when he heard one.

After the war, Tats's excellent English and familiarity with Western music made him a natural fit to manage the clubs at US military bases in Japan during the postwar American occupation. His club management experience—booking live entertainment for American GIs—led to managing Japanese jazz performers and forming an entertainment management agency in 1957.

While attending school as a boy in London, Tats had met Vic Lewis, who went on to become a jazz musician and music promoter in England. Vic sold his management business to Brian Epstein and thereafter became an Epstein associate at NEMS, helping Brian arrange international tours for the Beatles. In early 1966, as planning for the world tour was ramping up, Vic and Tats reconnected and discussed the possibility of bringing the Beatles to Japan. Although they had obstacles to overcome, Tats traveled to London to meet with Vic and Brian and begin the process of landing the biggest musical act in the world for its first performance in Tokyo.

Tats Nagashima (*left*) with Brian Epstein in Tokyo, 1966. *Photo: Robert Whitaker / Getty Images*

Negotiations between Tats and NEMS culminated in the April 26, 1966, contract signing in London for the Beatles to play in Japan. No venue was specified in the contract, but one of the principal conditions of the agreement was that any venue have a minimum of 10,000 seats. Japan had outdoor stadiums and arenas, but the concerts were scheduled for June and July—

Japan's rainy season—so an indoor venue was necessary. By process of elimination, the Budokan became the most logical choice, a decision that was, in the end, born of necessity. In a move he would soon regret, the Budokan's president agreed to host the Beatles' shows there, although he later claimed that he gave this permission before he knew about their long hair and the screaming girls who inevitably attended their performances.

The contracts had been signed, the approvals had been granted, and the shows would go on. Tats Nagashima had triumphed by setting himself up as the first musical promoter to bring the Beatles to Japan.

As publicity for the Beatles' forthcoming Budokan concerts spread, Tokyo society began to polarize. Right-wing conservatives began to foment a nationalist fervor over what they considered to be the desecration of a sacred Japanese shrine by hosting four long-haired musicians who would play Western music for crazed teens in an uninhibited rock-and-roll frenzy. Reports in Japanese media announced that right wingers wanted to kidnap the Beatles once they touched down in Japan to give them "proper haircuts."

Protests and denouncements became almost daily rituals leading up to the Beatles' five appearances at the Budokan, scheduled between June 30 and July 2. The anti-Beatles-at-the-Budokan demonstrations reached their zenith with a protest to be led by Japanese prime minister Eisaku Sato.

Although Prime Minister Sato was a member of Japan's pro-American Liberal Party and even won the Nobel Peace Prize in 1974 for his work against nuclear weapon proliferation, conservative Japanese nationalists pressured him to disavow the Beatles' planned appearances at the Budokan and publicly protest the impending shows. Three other notable Japanese citizens would join him in leading the protests, including Ryugen Hosokawa, a conservative journalist; respected octogenarian Matsutaro Shoriki; and the fourth handpicked protest leader—the most stunning member of what came to be known as the "drab four"—Tats Nagashima.

The man who himself had booked the Beatles in Tokyo and who had personally selected the Budokan as the concert venue was now going to stand shoulder to shoulder with Japan's prime minister to protest the very concerts he had arranged at the venue he had chosen.

Apparently, Tats's change of heart did not stop him from pocketing the substantial yen generated by the concerts' booming ticket sales.

By the time the Beatles touched down in the early hours of June 30, 1966, after a long delay caused by a typhoon (they didn't call it the rainy season for nothing), Japanese authorities had determined that the potential for unrest over the Budokan controversy, coupled with the fervor that followed the Beatles wherever they went, was more than their law enforcement and security officials could handle. If the situation got out of hand, it could give postwar Japan a black eye, which it could ill afford in the eyes of the world.

Authorities decided that the only way to control the potentially volatile situation was to essentially place the Beatles under house arrest in their hotel. Upon their arrival, they were hustled into official vehicles and whisked to the Tokyo Hilton. Despite their wishes to take in some of Tokyo's sights, the Beatles would be strictly confined to their hotel suite for the duration of their three-day visit—except, of course, when they were allowed to leave for their concerts. John and Paul—separately—managed to sneak out for brief periods (Paul through the main lobby, where he was promptly stopped by guards, and John, who had better success in his decampment, posing as a member of the press corps), but otherwise they would effectively remain shut-ins at the Hilton between their June 30 arrival and July 2 departure.

The Beatles played their first show at the Budokan at 6:30 p.m. on June 30, barely fifteen hours after landing in Tokyo. Although the reception was considered "warm," George recalled that the Japanese audiences were somewhat restrained, "a bit clinical," as he put it.

The Beatles performing at the Budokan, June 30, 1966, surrounded by security guards and kept far from their fans. *Photo: Robert Whitaker / Getty Images*

In reality, the Japanese authorities were concerned about snipers in the hall, among other potential dangers and disruptions, so they enforced strict rules that required all concertgoers to remain seated and stay out of the aisles. They confined seating to the mezzanine and upper balcony levels of the Budokan. No floor seating was permitted, and a cordon of police would ensure separation between the Beatles and their fans.

The relatively subdued reaction of the heavily policed audience meant that for the first time in years, the Beatles could actually hear themselves perform.

While the Beatles were imprisoned in the presidential suite at the Tokyo Hilton, they were visited by Tats Nagashima, the man who had both promoted and protested them. Tats came bearing gifts. He gave each Beatle a state-of-the-art Pentax camera. And, concerned that the boys might be bored while holed up at the Hilton, Tats also delivered painting supplies, including watercolor and oil paints and a large piece of white paper, to help the confined celebrities pass the time.

In addition to their talents as musicians and songwriters, the Beatles were able visual artists. As a schoolboy, John constantly drew cartoons and caricatures to accompany his witty stories of Lennonesque wordplay. After high school, he attended Liverpool College of Art, where he met both his first wife, Cynthia, and original Beatles bassist Stuart Sutcliffe. Paul, although not formally trained in visual arts, was no slouch with the paintbrush, going on to exhibit his works later in life. Ringo, too, in his post-Beatles life, painted pieces that turned up in galleries, and published several books of his photographs.

The Beatles working intently on their painting in the presidential suite of the Tokyo Hilton, July 1966. *Photo: Robert Whitaker / Getty Images*

The Beatles rolled out the 30-by-40-inch paper on a hotel table and placed a lamp in the center. With a mix of oil paints and watercolors, they began to work on the only painting produced by the four of them, aside from the walls and ceilings of the Casbah Club in Liverpool (see chapter 1).

After collaboratively painting a bright-colored background on the white paper, each Beatle took a corner to create his own contribution. According to witnesses, working on the painting became almost an obsession during their time in Tokyo. Photographer Robert Whitaker recalled that during their entire time on the 1966 world tour, the Beatles appeared the happiest and most contented while working on the group painting inside the Tokyo Hilton. Whitaker observed that "they'd stop, go and do a concert, and then it was 'Let's get back to the picture!'"

John and Paul painting in Tokyo. *Photo: Robert Whitaker / Getty Images*

The Beatles continued to work on their collective painting over the course of their three-night stay. John's and Paul's contributions appeared on the top of the elongated sheet, with Ringo's and George's at the bottom. As the finished project was described in the *Born Late* blog:

Paul's corner had a symmetrical, psychedelic feel, while John's had a dark center surrounded by thick oils. George's part of the picture was large and colorful, and Ringo's was cartoon-like.

It could be said that their individual contributions closely reflected their unique personalities.

Images of a Woman, oil and watercolor on paper, by John Lennon, Paul McCartney, George Harrison, and Ringo Starr, 1966. *Photo: Robert Whitaker / Getty Images*

When the Beatles completed the painting after their last shows on July 2, they removed the lamp that had been placed on the center of the paper to illuminate the undertaking, leaving a crisp, white circle in the center. Each Beatle signed his name adjacent to his contribution. The group named the painting *Images of a Woman*—even though no obvious image of a woman appears on the colorful work of art.

The completed painting ended up in the hands of Tetsusaburo Shimoyama, a movie theater owner who was also the president of the Beatles' Japanese fan club. Although some accounts say that the Beatles gave the painting to Shimoyama outright, others say that it was donated to a charity auction at which Shimoyama was the winning bidder. Either way, it is beyond dispute that he came to own the painting soon after its completion. In an interview for a 2020 piece in the *Japan Times*, Kimi Aida, Shimoyama's interpreter during the Beatles' 1966 visit, recalled seeing the painting in the Hilton while it was still wet, claiming that Shimoyama was given possession of it then and there.

Images of a Woman would remain on Japanese soil for most of the next half century. Although the Beatles collectively completed a colored-pencil sketch in 1967 as a sort of greeting-card apology to the organizers of the Monterey Pop Festival for declining their invitation to perform, no other collective work of visual art by all four Beatles is known to exist.

The Beatles, on their one and only visit to Japan as a band, found themselves at the center of a raging controversy not of their making. That controversy resulted in three days of involuntary confinement, but the contented Beatles turned their solitude into a collaborative creative pursuit and produced a singular work of art. *Images of a Woman* may not give Picasso a run for his money, but it stands alone as the one and only painting by the Beatles.

POSTSCRIPT

The Beatles had broken a virtual seal at the Budokan. The famed venue eventually hosted countless rock-and-roll concerts over the years. Many Americans first heard of the Budokan in 1979, when the breakthrough *Cheap Trick at Budokan* became one of the highest-selling live albums to ever climb the charts. *Rolling Stone* ranked it as number 13 on its list of the fifty greatest live albums of all time.

While holed up in the Tokyo Hilton, the Beatles had one other notable and enduring piece of creativity. After considering multiple titles for their forthcoming new LP, the band sent EMI a telegram from the hotel on July 2, informing them that they'd settled on a name for their new record: *Revolver*.

The Beatles left Tokyo on July 3, 1966, never to return as a band. They flew on to their next stop, Manila, the perilous pinnacle of their final tour. The story of the Beatles in the Philippines is an oft-told and well-known tale, but no chapter describing the 1966 world tour would be complete without a few highlights. The events in Manila would contribute, perhaps more than any, to the Beatles' decision to stop touring forever.

Upon their arrival in the Philippines, the Beatles were bizarrely whisked away to Manila Harbor, where they were inexplicably detained on a boat for hours before being taken to their hotel in the middle of the night. The press announced that on July 4, their first full day in the country, the Beatles would be the guests of Philippine president Ferdinand Marcos and his wife, Imelda, for a luncheon at the presidential palace. Everyone in Manila seemed to know about this reception—except the Beatles and their manager.

When government officials showed up to escort the Beatles to the presidential event, John, Paul, George, and Ringo, who understandably needed to rest, politely declined the invitation. What neither the Beatles nor Brian Epstein apparently knew at the time was that an "invitation" to the Marcos palace was not a request—it was a summons. The Marcos couple, at that time in office for only six months, did not yet have the well-deserved reputation they would earn over the years—that of murderous, dictatorial tyrants. Although the famous "snub" was not intentional, the damage had been done. (The Beatles had a general policy against diplomatic receptions ever since a guest at a party at the British embassy cut a lock of Ringo's hair on their first tour of America in 1964. "Bloody animals," John grumbled.)

The Beatles famously watched the local news coverage of their nonarrival at the presidential reception, complete with crying children and a noticeably frustrated Imelda Marcos, who huffed that her children preferred the Rolling Stones anyway.

When, in later years, the brutality of the Marcos regime became clear, Paul said, "We were glad to have done what we did. We must have been the only people who'd ever dared to snub Marcos!"

The Marcos regime exacted its revenge. After the Beatles completed their last show on July 4, they found they no longer had a police escort, and they were left to fend for themselves in getting back to the hotel. The following morning, as they were packing for their departure, multiple calls to order a room service breakfast were ignored. The famished Beatles made their way back to the airport, and tension mounted as they were first held in the transit lounge, famously hiding behind nuns for protection from the Marcos goons who had been sent to rough them up.

The Beatles and their entourage genuinely feared for their safety in the tense hours before their Manila departure. Once they finally settled into the British Airways jet, their temporary relief turned once again to fear as members of their traveling party were hauled off the plane. Before the Beatles would be allowed to leave, their manager was forced to pay a "leaving the Philippines tax" that was, not coincidentally, equal to the amount they had earned playing the two shows in Manila.

In other words, the Philippine authorities confiscated every cent the Beatles earned performing in their country. It turned out that snubbing Ferdinand and Imelda Marcos came at a price.

Perhaps more than any other single event, their experience in the Philippines soured the Beatles on touring. They never returned to the Philippine Islands. John said, "No plane is going to go through the Philippines with me on it. I wouldn't even fly over it. We'll just never go to any nuthouses again."

Another place the Beatles never returned to as a band was Japan. However, their individual experiences with the country did not end with the 1966 Beatles tour. John, of course, married Japanese native Yoko Ono, and together they visited Japan on several occasions to see her family and relax in the tranquil countryside of Karuizawa Province. More famously, on January 16, 1980, when Paul McCartney and Wings arrived in Tokyo for the eleven-day Japanese leg of their tour, Paul was arrested at the airport for possession of marijuana, which, at the time, was punishable by seven years in prison. After hours of interrogation and nine days in jail, he was released without charge, although he was on the hook to Japanese promoters for £1 million, owing to his inability to perform his contractual obligations.

Vic Lewis, the NEMS associate of Brian Epstein who had worked with Tats Nagashima on bringing the Beatles to Japan, died in London in 2009 at the age of eighty-nine after a long career as a musician, manager, and entrepreneur.

Tats Nagashima died in Tokyo on May 2, 1999, at the age of seventy-three after a bout with pneumonia. His passing was the subject of a short notice in the May 29, 1999, issue of *Billboard* magazine:

> The Japanese concert promoter was best-known for pioneering the appearances of foreign music acts, including the Beatles, in Japan. Nagashima got into the concert business in the mid-50s . . . he organized Japanese tours by a host of Western artists.

It seems like anyone with a Beatles connection will find it to be mentioned in the first line of their obituary as they head for the great concert hall in the sky.

After the death of Tetsusaburo Shimoyama, the Beatles' fan club president in Japan and original owner of *Images of a Woman*, his wife sold the painting to Takao Nishino, a Japanese record store owner who claimed he paid $280,000 for it in 1989. For three years, the painting hung in a humidity-controlled frame in his living room, after which he stored it under his bed for decades, save for the times he loaned it out for stories on Japanese television.

Nishino consigned the painting to Weiss Auctions, which on September 14, 2012, sold it to a bidder for $155,250. If Nishino's story about his acquisition is accurate, that amount was far less than what he paid for it in 1989. It is hard to imagine that such a rare Beatles' treasure would lose that much value in a collector's market that has long been frenzied, sending some auctions into the stratosphere for Beatles memorabilia and artifacts.

Furor continued to follow the Beatles on their 1966 tour as it reached America later in the summer. In Memphis, more death threats, religious protests, and the ominous presence of the KKK threatened to overshadow their performance in Memphis after John's "more popular than Jesus" remarks circulated in the South.

The Beatles at Candlestick Park in San Francisco during their last-ever live appearance, August 29, 1966. John fiddles with his Pentax camera while Paul looks through the lens of his. *Photo: Koh Hasebe / Shinko Music / Getty Images*

Although the fans in Candlestick Park in San Francisco did not know it at the time, nor did the rest of the world, the last ticketed Beatles concert our planet would ever host took place on August 29, 1966, at the conclusion of their tumultuous world tour. The Beatles, however, *did* know it would be their final show, since they had already agreed as a band to stop touring. Wanting to memorialize the event, the Beatles took their own pictures of the San Francisco show as personal keepsakes.

In photos from the conclusion of this final concert at Candlestick, one can clearly see some of the Beatles holding their Pentax cameras while they were walking between the stage and their dressing room.

The very same cameras given to them in Japan by Mr. Tats Nagashima.

CHAPTER 12

"HERE COME OLD FLAT TOP ..."
How "Come Together" Entangled a Beatle with a Mobster

On the opening track of *Abbey Road*, John Lennon sings the immortal line "Here come old flat top, he come grooving up slowly," words he admitted borrowing—with slight adjustments—from the old Chuck Berry tune "You Can't Catch Me." Even though such homages by recording artists to their musical influences were commonplace, the owner of Berry's song copyrights was not amused. As it turned out, this particular cranky copyright owner was a notorious, mob-connected wiseguy.

This is the story of how John's derivative lyrics in one of the most popular Beatles songs of all time drew him into a seven-year tangle with a mobster and how he finally broke free.

Soon after the release of *Abbey Road* in September 1969, John Lennon gave an interview in which he acknowledged the influence of Chuck Berry on his new song, the sexually charged "Come Together." It had never been a secret that Berry was an outsized influence on the Beatles. They had recorded several Berry covers for studio albums and played even more of his songs in their live sets and numerous BBC performances.

In fact, "Come Together" even featured a line borrowed nearly verbatim from Berry: "Here come old flat top, he come grooving up slowly," from the 1956 classic "You Can't Catch Me." Berry had written, "Here come a flat top, he was moving up with me" after being overtaken by a couple of dudes with crew cuts on the New Jersey Turnpike.

Recorded music is replete with examples of artists using borrowed lines, snippets of chord progressions, and tasty riffs from their musical heroes. Countless artists lifted liberally from the Beatles' body of work. The Beatles did it too, and so has every recording artist who ever put tracks on tape. After all, there are only seven musical notes in the entire sonic universe of Western music; twelve when you throw in the sharps and flats in between. Words are more plentiful, but finite. It is a mathematical inevitability that musicians will repeat words, notes, and chords that others have used somewhere along the line.

John Lennon with Chuck Berry, 1972. *Photo: Mediapunch/Shutterstock*

John Lennon paid musical tribute to Chuck Berry by using a few lines of a lyric and a Berryesque chord progression in "Come Together." During early rehearsals, Paul even suggested that John make changes to the song that would put some distance between "You Can't Catch Me" and the new Lennon and McCartney composition. John apparently considered the Chuck Berry influence in "Come Together" to be an innocent tribute.

Innocent homage notwithstanding, Morris "Mo" Levy knew a shakedown opportunity when he heard one.

Mo Levy was a New York tough guy, born in 1927 and reared on the streets of Harlem. After assaulting a teacher and being tossed out of school at age thirteen, Levy hung around seedy nightclubs, performed odd jobs, served a tour in the Navy, and returned to New York to make his bones. With the backing of the Genovese crime family, Levy and several partners used mob money to buy the Manhattan club Birdland and turned it into one of New York's premier jazz clubs.

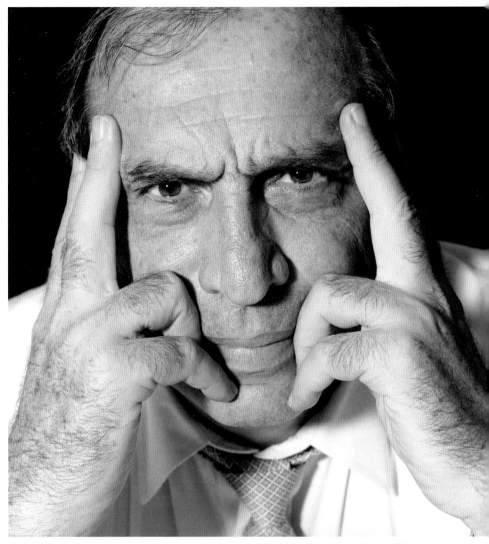

You lookin' at me? Music industry wiseguy Morris Levy. *Photo: Deborah Feingold / Corbis / Getty Images*

One night at Birdland, a representative of the American Society of Composers, Authors and Publishers (ASCAP) approached Mo Levy and requested payment for performance royalties of songs the club's cover bands had performed. Having never heard of ASCAP (an organization that, to this day, represents songwriters and copyright holders), the wiseguy naturally believed the demands for payment were merely attempted shakedowns by a rival crime family. After consulting with his lawyer, Levy learned that ASCAP was the real deal, and that venues such as Birdland were required to pay for the rights to perform live versions of tunes owned by publishers.

After grudgingly handing over the ASCAP bounty, Levy realized there must be money in owning music-publishing rights. He swiftly put his laundered mob profits to work, buying up the rights to jazz and early rock-and-roll songs, often for relatively small sums to cash-strapped composers. Perhaps some of these purchases resulted from offers the owners simply couldn't refuse.

Levy set up a publishing company called Patricia Music (named after his wife) and ultimately staged a hostile takeover of Roulette Records. Levy consolidated his growing music industry interests into a company called Big Seven Music Corp. Through Big Seven, Levy contracted to print covers and press records for smaller labels, often stealing their music and selling his own unauthorized versions. Levy also managed to revise the songwriting credits on many of the tunes he came to own, adding himself as a cowriter of songs he had no hand in creating. Levy leveraged these and other tactics to swindle artists, record companies, and other music copyright holders out of the royalties due them.

Levy took singer Tommy James (of Tommy James and the Shondells fame) under his corrupt wing and helped guide him to stardom in the 1960s. James later wrote a book about his experiences with Levy called *Me, the Mob, and the Music: One Helluva Ride with Tommy James and the Shondells.*

Mo Levy (*second from left*) with Tommy James (*seated*), July 1969. *Photo: Don Paulsen / Michael Ochs Archives / Getty Images*

In the course of his music industry acquisitions, Levy obtained the rights to "You Can't Catch Me" from payola vet Alan Freed, the disc jockey who has been spuriously credited with coining the term "rock and roll." So, with the copyright in his pocket and John Lennon's public quasi-confession of "borrowing" from the Berry tune, Levy cunningly connected the dots that he hoped would lead to deep Beatle pockets. Not long after *Abbey Road*'s release in 1969, Levy filed a lawsuit alleging copyright infringement by Lennon in "Come Together," and John Lennon's involuntary association with the mob began.

In the fall of 1973, with the Levy lawsuit still hanging over his head during the Los Angeles phase of John's "Lost Weekend," he had the itch to record an album of rock oldies. He had, at least temporarily, grown weary of being the composer *and* performer of his songs. John found the idea of simply being a musician and a singer, without bearing the additional burdens of a composer/arranger, to be appealing.

John's desire to get back to his rock roots afforded an opportunity to resolve the long-standing Mo Levy litigation. At the time, the solution seemed to be ingenious: For his next album, John would record three songs from Levy's publishing catalog, which contained an ample supply of rock oldies that appealed to John's quest for nostalgic, roots-era rock and roll. It would cost him nothing to record the songs, and the sales that would be generated by a John Lennon record would amply compensate Mo Levy for his troubles. This framework to free John from Levy's mob clutches must have appealed to John, and he signed a settlement agreement promising to record the Levy-owned tunes.

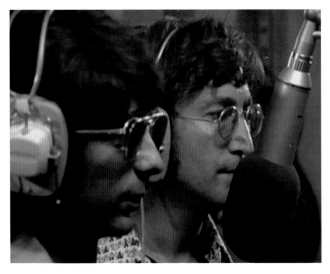

Phil Spector (*left*) with John Lennon in Los Angeles. *Photo: BBC Arena / Vixpix / Kobal / Shutterstock*

The L.A. recording sessions that ensued were produced by Phil Spector. With Phil Spector came the inevitable chaos associated with Phil Spector. Among the tracks recorded in these alcohol-and-cocaine-fueled sessions were three Big Seven songs—"Angel Baby," "Ya Ya," and the original offender, "You Can't Catch Me."

In a Spectorian drama that accompanied the famed but troubled record producer wherever he went, Phil Spector walked out of the sessions and took custody of the master tapes. Soon thereafter, he was in a car accident, which he claimed left him seriously injured. He refused the requests of John and Capitol Records to return the masters, and, at the time, it appeared as though the sessions and the confiscated tapes would yield no releasable material.

While the L.A. master tapes were still in limbo, John returned to New York. His creative compositional juices flowing once again, he began writing, arranging, and recording the songs for his forthcoming album, *Walls and Bridges*. It was released in late September 1974 and, once again John became entangled with the disgruntled don.

Mo Levy was furious that a new John Lennon album had dropped *without* the three Big Seven songs he had promised to include on his "next" album as part of the 1973 settlement agreement (*Walls and Bridges* did contain a one-minute "snippet" of "Ya Ya," but it was not nearly enough to satisfy Levy or the terms of the settlement agreement). After phoning John's lawyer to demand a meeting, Levy, Lennon, and the attorney met in New York on October 8, 1974. John explained that he had, in fact, in good faith recorded the tracks as promised, but that Phil Spector had then absconded with the master tapes containing the obligatory Big Seven songs. John told Levy that he would summon the *Walls and Bridges* musicians, return to the studio, and rerecord his oldies album from scratch.

The mobster was mollified for the moment. In fact, Levy went so far as to offer John and his band the use of his upstate New York farm to rehearse for the upcoming sessions. After relentless pestering by Levy, John obliged. Levy also offered John the use of his vacation condo in Palm Beach, and he availed himself of that on a Christmas 1974 Florida vacation with son Julian and May Pang (see chapter 14).

In the meantime, Capitol Records paid Phil Spector a ransom of $90,000 in cash and retrieved the L.A. rock-and-roll oldies master tapes. After relistening to the recordings, John and his label were largely dissatisfied with what they heard. The tracks sounded overproduced (a common complaint attached to Spector's work), and John's alcohol-soaked voice was not in its best form. Only four of the eight songs on the L.A. session tapes and only one of the Big Seven tunes were deemed to be usable.

Although not entirely pleased with the results, John and his band managed to record nine tracks, including two Big Seven numbers, in a two-week studio sprint. Coupled with the four "usable" Spector-produced tracks, John finally had enough material in the can for his oldies album. Confident that Mo Levy would consider the completion of the album as a further gesture of good faith on his part, John sent Levy a second-generation copy of the tapes for his perusal. John maintained that the purpose of sending the tapes to Levy was merely to show him that John had done what he promised to do, and that John was finally in position to satisfy his 1973 settlement agreement with Levy once and for all.

But nothing is ever that simple for a Beatle. And John's gesture of goodwill in sending Levy the tapes opened John up to a new line of litigation. No good deed ever goes unpunished.

Levy claimed that during the October 8 meeting, John had verbally promised to let him release his planned rock oldies album on his own record label, Adam VIII Limited, one of the ubiquitous 1970s TV/mail-order companies that sold everything from record albums to the Popeil Pocket Fisherman ("Call now! Operators are standing by!"). You would think that a Mafia wiseguy of Levy's stature would be well aware that John was in no position to grant him the rights to release an album when he was already under contract to Capitol Records in the US and EMI elsewhere. You'd also think that an artist who had been around the block, as John clearly had, would know his limitations to assign such rights in the first place—if things had even happened the way Levy claimed. But Levy was steadfast in maintaining that John had verbally granted him the rights to release his rock-and-roll oldies album.

Capitol Records, which already had $90,000 tied up in the ransom it paid Phil Spector to retrieve the L.A. session tapes, was absolutely unwilling to grant Mo Levy the right to release a John Lennon solo record, especially containing tracks that Capitol itself had paid to produce.

In February 1975, Mo Levy was not about to let a small detail like Capitol Records' refusal to release its contractual rights to one of the world's biggest recording artists stand in the way of recouping his pound of flesh for John Lennon's unforgivable sin of singing the line "Here come old flat top" back in 1969.

Mo Levy held an ace card—the copy of the oldies tape that John had naively sent him a few months before. Dissatisfied with Capitol Records' refusal and eager to cash in, Levy decided to hastily press his inferior-quality recordings onto vinyl, shove them into hastily designed album sleeves, and run late-night ads in a few East Coast cities for a brand-new John Lennon album:

JOHN LENNON SINGS THE GREAT ROCK AND ROLL HITS: ROOTS

AVAILABLE NOW FROM ADAM VIII! $4.98 PER RECORD / $5.98 PER TAPE. OPERATORS ARE STANDING BY!

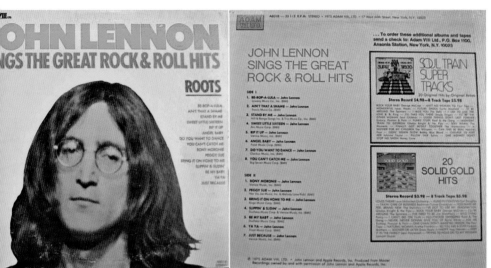

The *Roots* album cover. *Photo: Doug Wolfberg*

Levy pressed 3,000 copies and sold about half before Capitol Records' lawyers shut him down, going after the television stations that ran Levy's ads and enjoining Levy directly.

Capitol Records, in the few days after Levy rush-released *Roots*, hurriedly brought to market its own "legitimate" Lennon album, simply titled *Rock 'n' Roll*. So, after more than a year of delay, marked by drunken L.A. sessions, master tapes held hostage, and a menacing mobster, not one but *two* albums of rock oldies by John Lennon appeared abruptly on the music market.

In the final assembly of *Rock 'n' Roll* for its brisk February 1975 release, Capitol dropped "Angel Baby," one of the Big Seven songs slated for the album, from the final track listing. This meant *Rock 'n' Roll* contained only two—and not the requisite three—Levy-owned compositions, opening the door for what was sure to be another round of Levy litigation.

Sure enough, Levy obliged.

Among other claims, Levy sued John for failing to uphold his three-song "Come Together" settlement agreement and breaching his alleged oral promise to allow Levy to sell his oldies album on the Adam VIII label.

At first, Levy claimed the "verbal contract" gave him rights to distribute the record worldwide; he subsequently amended the lawsuit to assert a more limited agreement that the rights John granted were for US distribution only. Levy claimed damages of more than $40 million. John countersued, claiming that Levy's use of an inferior recording and shoddy packaging (including a long-haired photo of John from 1968 on the cover) was of such poor quality that it damaged his reputation.

In a clever move and to accentuate the point that the 1968 long-haired photo was the wrong choice for an album of 1950s rock-and-roll classics, John showed up to the January 1976 trial with newly shorn, short hair. When Levy's attorney cross-examined him on the witness stand, accusing him of having cut his hippie hair solely for trial appearances, John, ever the Liverpudlian comedian, elicited laughs from everyone in the courtroom (judge included) when he answered, "Rubbish. I cut it every eighteen months."

The judge in the Levy-Lennon lawsuit issued his decision on February 20, 1976, ruling that Levy failed to establish that an oral contract existed. Noting that Levy had needed to amend his complaint to state and then restate the terms of the alleged verbal contract, the judge wrote the following:

> The fact that Levy . . . [has] experienced such difficulty in formulating the terms of the contract for presentation to the court is sufficient in itself to cast doubt on whether there was ever a contract at all. . . . I conclude, on the basis of the October 8, 1974, meeting and on the basis of all the other relevant evidence, that no contract was entered into by Lennon . . . granting Levy . . . the right to produce and distribute Lennon's rock[-]and[-]roll album.

After all the claims were resolved and the case was reviewed by a US appeals court, the final rulings on April 13, 1977, were

$49,912.96 to Lennon for lost royalties

$35,000 to Lennon for injury to reputation

$6,795 damages to Levy / Big Seven for breach of the "Come Together" settlement agreement

So, with a net gain of $78,117.96, John Lennon was finally free of mobster Mo Levy, seven years and seven months after the release of *Abbey Road* and its leadoff track, "Come Together," with its simple, "Here come old flat top," lyrical homage to Chuck Berry.

POSTSCRIPT

In a rich piece of irony, later legal commentators have noted that the "original sin" in the Mo Levy affair, the use of the line "Here come old flat top" in "Come Together," was *not*, in fact, copyright infringement under the law. They claim that it was a mistake for John Lennon to have entered into a settlement agreement with Levy over such thin allegations of plagiarism.

Legal observer Trip Aldredge wrote in 2019 that Levy would likely not have prevailed in the original "Come Together" infringement lawsuit, noting that the "fair use" doctrine would have been a viable defense. In fact, this doctrine, which allows in certain instances the use of portions of copyrighted work without permission from the owner, was such a potent defense in cases like this that it later was enacted into federal statutory law.

Nevertheless, perhaps weary of the morass into which his former bandmate George Harrison had seemingly fallen over plagiarism allegations surrounding his hit "My Sweet Lord," John likely believed that settling quickly and quietly with Mo Levy was the wisest course of action. It was, of course, this settlement that gave rise to the Big Seven three-song promise and the lingering presence of Mo Levy in John's life.

Incidentally, Paul's father-in-law, Lee Eastman, the entertainment industry lawyer whom Paul unsuccessfully lobbied the Beatles to retain as their representative (and who represented Paul individually), wisely extricated Paul from the "Come Together" mess by pinning down John to admit sole authorship and thus obtaining, in essence, an indemnification agreement on behalf of his client. Even though legal authorship of the published song was credited to "Lennon and McCartney," Eastman, a wise and by all accounts highly competent lawyer, effectively hung out to dry the Lennon half of the compositional partnership. Other than the interest that Paul had as one of the owners of Apple and Maclen Music, which were putative codefendants in the Levy litigation, Paul escaped Levy's legal tractor beam through his father-in-law's jurisprudential acumen.

The *Rock 'n' Roll* album turned out to be one of the lowest-selling records of John's solo career, selling only about a quarter of the number of copies that *Imagine* sold. In fact, *Rock 'n' Roll* was the last John Lennon release for a five-year stretch; he decided to withdraw from the music business to focus on his newly born son, Sean, and become a self-described househusband, while Yoko tended to the family's business interests.

It is no wonder that the protracted and tortured history of recording, litigating, releasing, and relitigating his album of rock oldies took its toll on John Lennon. By most accounts, his five-year hiatus was a period of relative domestic tranquility and happiness, which he richly deserved.

John's withdrawal from the music business in 1975 made the November 1980 release of *Double Fantasy* that much more special; one of popular music's cornerstone artists was back. Of course, in perhaps the most sorrowful rock-and-roll epitaph ever, John Lennon's comeback—and his life—ended tragically just weeks after the release of this heavily anticipated album.

The Adam VIII album *Roots*, with only 3,000 printed copies, became a prized acquisition among Lennon collectibles. Although numerous re-pressed forgeries abound, authentic copies have sold for thousands of dollars.

The juiciest postscript is the story of Mo Levy.

In 1975, Levy and a mob colleague, Nathan "Big Nat" McCalla, were charged with assaulting an off-duty police officer, who lost an eye in the attack. Levy beat the rap on that charge, but his associate, Big Nat, was murdered in Florida in 1980.

Levy was later the subject of a prolonged FBI investigation related to the infiltration of organized crime into the record business. A mob turncoat led authorities to Levy's unsavory arrangements, testified against him, and entered the federal witness protection program. Levy came to be known as "the godfather of the American music business."

During this investigation, which began in 1984, the feds uncovered evidence of Levy's involvement in an extortion plot and assault against a record wholesaler in Pennsylvania. Much of the evidence against Levy was gathered through FBI wiretaps, including from a mic placed in a sign behind Levy's desk that said "O Lord! Give me a Bastard with talent!" (the mic was surreptitiously placed inside the "O"). Delicious irony.

The FBI investigation culminated in the much-publicized September 1986 arrest of Levy in Boston, with the suspect forced to perp walk before the cameras while holding—what else?—a record album to hide the handcuffs. Levy took to the airwaves to defend himself, notably giving a national interview the following day to NBC's investigative reporter Brian Ross. When Ross asked Levy about alleged connections between organized crime and the music business, Levy's response was classic mob gold: "There is no connection between the mob and the music business."

Levy's denial would likely been more credible had he not delivered it in his best New York mob voice of gravel and bravado, with his classic slicked-back gangster hairdo and shifty eyes. Levy looked and sounded every inch the mobster he was, straight out of central casting for a Martin Scorsese film. In fact, it was said that Levy served as the inspiration for a character on the East Coast Mafia TV drama, *The Sopranos*.

The investigation also uncovered evidence that Levy's music industry businesses were a mere Mafia front, part of the tried-and-true mob method of laundering illicit profits through seemingly legitimate companies. In Levy's case, he was fronting for Genovese crime family boss Vincent "the Chin" Gigante.

Levy went to trial in 1988 and was convicted that December of two counts of extortion and conspiracy. He was sentenced to ten years in prison but remained free on bail during his appeal. His bail, ironically, was secured by the New York farm at which Levy had hosted John Lennon and his band during rehearsals for the *Rock 'n' Roll* album in 1974.

After exhausting his appeals, with his conviction upheld, Levy was finally ordered to report to prison and begin serving his sentence on July 16, 1990.

Mo Levy managed to avoid prison by dying of cancer on May 20, 1990.

Levy's legacy continued to shadow his family for decades. In 2012, New Jersey authorities held up the licensing of a medical marijuana company because one of the principals was Levy's son, Adam.

John Lennon was raised without a father and had met the freeloading Alfred "Freddie" Lennon on only a few occasions. It has been said that as a result, John was attracted to colorful "father figures"—men such as Mo Levy, Allen Klein, the Maharishi, and a cast of other advisers, managers, peaceniks, producers, posers, and gurus over the course of his career—men who, inevitably, would let him down in the end.

Some of John Lennon's more questionable associations produced some of the most colorful but turbulent stories of his life. A nearly eight-year association with one of the twentieth century's larger-than-life East Coast mail-order Mafia figures, all because of a simple line in a legendary song, constituted a confluence of events that seemingly could happen only to John Lennon.

CHAPTER 13

A TOOT AND A SNORE IN '74

The Last Lennon–McCartney Recordings

In early 1974, the scabs covering the wounds of the Beatles' breakup were once again starting to bleed. Paul and John were publicly feuding through song lyrics and had not laid eyes on one another in three years.

John's personal life in New York was also spiraling out of control, with his wife setting him up with a mistress and showing him the door. While living a life of excess in Los Angeles, John found himself in a recording studio, eyeball to eyeball with the one person in the world he would least expect. This is the story of the final Lennon–McCartney recording session, the unreleased and unlistenable music that resulted, and how it produced a long-awaited reunion—although not the one Beatles fans had hoped for.

"Valiant Paul McCartney, I presume?"

"Sir Jasper Lennon, I presume"?

This exchange of greetings in March 1974 marked the first time John Lennon and Paul McCartney had seen each other in three years. It would also be the last time, two nights later, they would ever record music together.

The two most famous and successful songwriters and musicians in rock-and-roll history—childhood friends now estranged by acrimony, business disputes, and litigation—were brought face to face by the unexpected and unannounced arrival of Paul and Linda McCartney at Burbank Studios in Los Angeles. There, John had been holed up with his drinking buddy Harry Nilsson while producing his new album, *Pussy Cats*. John's cryptic greeting of "Valiant Paul McCartney" was a Beatle insider joke. Paul instantly knew its meaning and responded in kind.

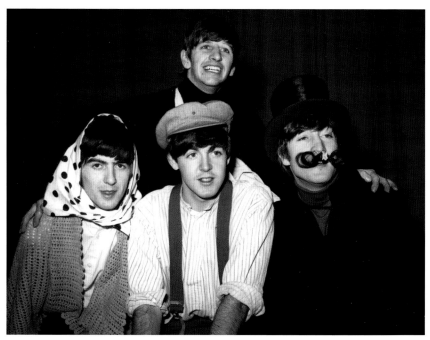

"Sir Jasper Lennon" and "Valiant Paul the Signalman," along with Ringo and George, in costume for their 1963 Christmas special. *Photo: PA Images / Getty Images*

"Valiant Paul" the Signalman and Sir Jasper Lennon were the names of their characters in a Beatles Christmas special Brian Epstein had produced way back in 1963. So much had happened to them since then.

The breakup of the Beatles as a working band occurred in 1969, but their breakup as a legal partnership remained on hold. Business and financial disputes still permeated the relationship among the four ex-Beatles, and the resulting tension and discord hung in the air like the chords of an out-of-tune guitar.

The strain among the Beatles was most acute between John and Paul. Creative rivalry between the two had fueled their unparalleled output of compositions between 1962 and 1970. However, that rivalry turned bitter. Instead of competing with each other as songwriters for the collective good of a band, they now channeled their creative energies into a distastefully public spectacle of bitterness and recrimination.

Most notoriously, John and Paul hurled thinly veiled, hurtful insults at each other in the press and in their songs.

Paul began the back and forth of bitterness with his 1971 tune "Too Many People," which was featured on his 1971 album *Ram*, and on the B side of the "Uncle Albert / Admiral Halsey" single.

Piss off, cake.

Too many people preaching practices.

You took your lucky break and broke it in two.

John heard these lines as a direct assault on him and Yoko. Paul did not deny it.

In later interviews, he outright confessed to these lyrical swipes at his old partner.

He's been doing a lot of preaching, and it got up my nose a little bit. [It] was a little dig at John and Yoko.

I felt John and Yoko were telling everyone what to do. And I felt we didn't need to be told what to do. The whole tenor of the Beatles thing had been, like, to each his own. Freedom. Suddenly it was "You should do this." It was just a bit of the wagging finger, and I was pissed off with it. So that one got to be a thing about them.

Although Paul clearly was taking his shots at John, he at least wrapped his references in semiobscure lyrics that much of the public might have missed, had the feud not escalated. Paul and Linda also included a photo in a music industry publication of them dressed as clowns in bags, another industry-insider jab at John and Yoko.

John Lennon was not one to be outdone when his caustic wit met with righteous indignation. He went nuclear.

John responded to Paul's lyrical and photographic swipes with an even bolder and more direct attack on his former best friend. John's response took the form of biting lyrics in his own 1971 tune "How Do You Sleep," from the *Imagine* album.

So Sgt. Pepper took you by surprise.

Those freaks was right when they said you was dead.

The only thing you done was [Y]esterday. And since you're gone you're just another day.

How do you sleep. How do you sleep at night.

In a rehearsal of the song filmed during the recording of *Imagine*, John added words to the chorus, lest anyone miss his point: "*How do you sleep, you c**t.*"

Not only had John called out two of Paul's songs by name ("Yesterday" and "Another Day"), but he had gained the tacit support of another Beatle in his counterassault on Paul: the unmistakable slide guitar work of George Harrison featured prominently on the track.

John later admitted that "How Do You Sleep" was "an answer" to "Too Many People," but when pressed in interviews, he backed off the direct lyrical lobs he had launched against Paul. He claimed that he had used his relationship with Paul merely as creative fodder for a piece of music that stood independent of their simmering feud, even backpedaling so far as to imply that he actually was writing about himself. But most people did not buy John's efforts to deny the attack. Even the subject of the pointed barbs admitted they had found their mark. "Those things were pretty hurtful," Paul admitted.

A web of litigation also encircled the Beatles. The public clamored for a Beatles reunion, but as Paul's father-in-law, entertainment lawyer Lee Eastman, had made clear, no such reunion could be contemplated until John, Paul, George, and Ringo could bury their intertwined and acrimonious business and legal disputes and find some form of global resolution.

John and Yoko's marriage was also falling apart in the summer of 1973. Yoko later admitted that being the target of the world's hate for her perceived role in the demise of the Beatles was beginning to suffocate her. "I needed a rest. I needed space," she would later say of that time. "Can you imagine every day of getting this vibration from people of hate? You want to get out of that."

Yoko told John she wanted a separation. But she also believed he would need someone to look after him, even to fulfill his sexual needs in her absence. Recognizing that John was attracted to their personal assistant, she gave the twenty-two-year-old an unusual new assignment: become John's lover.

May Pang began working at the offices of ABKCO Music & Records in 1970. ABKCO was the New York office of Allen Klein, the controversial music industry heavyweight with a dubious reputation who had taken over representation of three of the four Beatles and management of their Apple company. When John and Yoko moved to New York in 1971, May became John and Yoko's personal assistant, doing everything from running personal errands to organizing art exhibitions of Yoko's work.

By late 1972 and early 1973, May could sense growing strain between her two bosses. "It was a very strange period for John and Yoko," she told an interviewer in 2017. "You could feel the tension between them." May said that one day Yoko walked into her office and confided that "John and

I are not getting along. He's probably going to start seeing other people." She also recalled Yoko's directness in what came next: "You don't have a boyfriend . . . I think you would be good for him."

Despite May's protestation that she was not interested, John leaned over and kissed her as the two later rode an elevator. "I've been waiting to do this all day," he told her. May ultimately found it impossible to resist what she characterized as John's persistent pursuit.

Yoko showed John the door, and he took up residence with May in an apartment on East 52nd Street in Manhattan.

Thus began what John described as his "lost weekend," an eighteen-month period of his life that included separation from Yoko, a long-term affair with May, three albums, and storied rock-and-roll excess and mayhem.

In October 1973, just a few months into the lost weekend, John and May left New York for Los Angeles for what was supposed to be a short promotional trip for John's new album, *Mind Games*. They decided to stay in L.A. for an extended time, and it wasn't long before John renewed friendships with some of the 1970s most notorious purveyors of rock-and-roll debauchery. Keith Moon and Harry Nilsson were the notable standouts in this scandalous crew.

John Lennon and May Pang in a public display of affection, with a hard-drinking Harry Nilsson in the foreground, Troubadour Club, Los Angeles, March 12, 1974. *Photo: Michael Ochs Archives / Getty Images*

John recorded tracks for a rock oldies album with the colorful and ultimately quite dangerous Phil Spector as producer (see chapter 12). Those legendary, alcohol-soaked sessions circuitously led to the *Rock 'n' Roll* album. They also involved Spector firing a gun at the ceiling of the recording studio in just one of many presages of a violent, firearm-obsessed future that ultimately landed him in prison for murder for the remainder of his life, which came to an end in early 2021.

In March 1974, Harry Nilsson kept the party going by asking John to produce his new album, *Pussy Cats*. Recording began early in the month at Burbank Studios.

On March 12, 1974, one of the more famous episodes of the lost weekend became an instant and inescapable part of Lennon lore. While taking in a Smothers Brothers musical comedy performance at the Troubadour club (where, on another occasion, he had paraded around with a sanitary pad on his head), a drunken John relentlessly heckled Tom and Dick Smothers, who had been friends from the 1960s, during their act. This prompted the club's manager to show Lennon the door.

John Lennon and Harry Nilsson being ejected from the Troubadour Club, March 12, 1974. *Photo: Maureen Donaldson / Getty Images*

A few weeks later, John was in the studio with Nilsson working on *Pussy Cats*, when two unexpected visitors stopped in: his long-estranged friends, Paul and Linda McCartney.

Despite all the lawyers, lawsuits, arguments, and acrimony between them, much of which had spilled over into song lyrics and newspaper articles, after John saw Paul and they exchanged their "Valiant/Jasper" greetings, it was as if the two old friends picked up right where they had left off. After an initial tinge of awkward tension in the room, John and Paul appeared to fall right back into an old, easy friendship. Witnesses recall being happy to see the rapport between the two living legends. They planned to meet again in the studio a couple of nights later, on March 28.

Also present in the studio when Paul came back on the twenty-eighth was an array of musical luminaries that included Nilsson, Stevie Wonder, Jesse Ed Davis, Bobby Keys, and producer Ed Freeman. But there was absolutely no doubt about which musicians were the focus of the session: "There were fifty other people playing," Lennon would later say with some exaggeration, but "all [were] just watching me and Paul."

What do some of the world's most talented musicians do when they find themselves together in a recording studio?

They jam. And since it is 1974, they also snort a lot of cocaine.

Paul took up a perch behind the drum kit. Stevie Wonder played electric piano, and Linda McCartney played organ. May Pang rattled a tambourine, while Jesse Ed Davis and John played guitar. Producer Freeman filled in on bass. Bobby Keys played sax. Nilsson, Lennon, McCartney, and Wonder all sang.

The tape started rolling.

At the start of the session, John can be heard offering Stevie Wonder the coke that was going around the studio. Obviously, it had already made multiple passes, and it would make several more over the course of the session.

"You wanna snort, Steve? A toot? It's goin' around."

What resulted from the course of the alcohol-and-cocaine-fueled recording session was, as the tapes reveal, a musical train wreck.

Although the session was essentially a loose, disorganized jam consisting of song fragments as opposed to a serious attempt at recording usable material, the "official" track listing included the following:

"Bluesy Jam"
"Lucille"
"Nightmares"
"Stand by Me"
Medley: "Cupid," "Chain Gang," and "Take This Hammer"

The recordings were never released. In fact, the public didn't even know that John and Paul had met up, let alone recorded together in a studio. It wasn't until 1975 that John somewhat casually revealed the existence of the session during an interview: "I did actually play with Paul. We did a lot of stuff in L.A." Confirmation of a recording came in 1983, with May Pang's book *Loving John*. Paul referred to the session in a 1997 interview, remarking only that "the session was hazy . . . for a number of reasons."

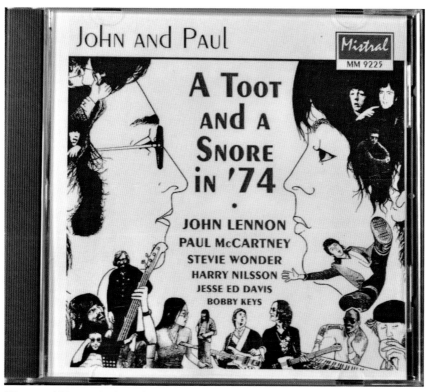

CD cover, *A Toot and a Snore in '74*. Photo: Doug Wolfberg

A twenty-eight-minute bootleg, complete with *Revolver*-style artwork, began to circulate in 1992. Other than its historical value as the only Lennon and McCartney recording session between *Abbey Road* in 1969 and John's death in 1980, it holds no significant musical or artistic value.

The name given to the recording of this hazy, musically inept, nearly forgotten studio session?

A Toot and a Snore in '74.

POSTSCRIPT

The most tantalizing postscript to the *Toot and a Snore* session was how close the world came to a Beatles studio reunion in March 1974. It turns out that *all four* Beatles were in L.A.

George Harrison was recording at A&M Studios with his Indian music guru, Ravi Shankar. The drummer on Harry Nilsson's *Pussy Cats* album was none other than Ringo Starr. In fact, it was Ringo's drum kit that Paul commandeered for the *Toot and a Snore* session.

"Paul always messes up my drums!" Ringo would complain the following day.

Although John and Ringo hung out during the lost weekend, George made a point of avoiding his former bandmates while they all inhabited the same city. George embarked on an American tour later in 1974, the first for any solo Beatle. Although his Dark Horse tour featured several talented musicians, George's voice was strained, and the shows were almost universally panned by critics. He would never again tour America.

While John and Paul were together in L.A., they had made tentative plans for John to come to New Orleans in early 1975, when Paul was planning to record material for what became his *Venus and Mars* album. Talk of a Beatles reunion started to gain traction in the music press.

But a reunion of another sort would supersede any attempt at a second Lennon and McCartney studio reunion, or a Beatles reunion, for that matter. And Paul became the unexpected catalyst.

While Yoko visited with Paul and Linda during a trip to London during the lost weekend, she confided that she wanted John back, although only under the condition that they would start slowly, basically "dating" again. Paul delivered this message to John in L.A.

It is ironic—and touching—that Paul would facilitate the reunion of his best friend and the woman whom many, including Paul himself, scorned in the waning days of the Beatles.

The planned studio reunion of John and Paul in New Orleans never took place. They did, however, resume regular communication and even see each other several times before John's death in 1980. Sadly, they never again recorded music together. According to Paul, they had fully reconciled in conversations prior to the unthinkable events of December 8, 1980. In interviews to this day, Paul expresses gratitude for having patched things up with his former bandmate before his death.

John returned to Yoko in New York in early 1975 and soon thereafter returned to their home at the Dakota, a Victorian-era building in New York City. One happy product of their reconciliation, son Sean, was born on John's thirty-fifth birthday, October 9, 1975. With Yoko's support, John realized that he did not have to be continuously running on the rock-and-roll treadmill to have a fulfilling life. He withdrew from the music business to find domestic bliss at home, becoming a full-time father and helping to run the household while Yoko took care of their business interests.

John remained with Yoko for the rest of his life.

After a short life of brilliant talent but excessive behavior, Harry Nilsson died of an apparent heart attack in L.A. on January 15, 1994. He was fifty-two.

May Pang went on to write several Lennon-themed books, including *Loving John* in 1983 and *Instamatic Karma*, a 2008 book of her personal photographs from the lost weekend. She married record producer Tony Visconti in 1989 and had two children prior to their divorce in 2000. Rumors abounded that she sporadically renewed her affair with John, and she readily admits that they remained in touch until his death. She became close friends with John's first wife, Cynthia, and since the mid-1970s has bumped into Yoko Ono only once by happenstance. She still lives in New York.

Over the years, May Pang has adamantly maintained that the lost weekend was not all "lost." She points out, accurately, that John Lennon turned out three albums, *Mind Games*, *Walls and Bridges*, and *Rock 'n' Roll*, during this period and even scored his first—and only—number 1 solo hit during his lifetime, the Elton John duet "Whatever Gets You through the Night."

May is correct that the lost weekend turned out some memorable music. Although, sadly, *A Toot and a Snore in '74* cannot, by any measure, be counted as "memorable music," it stands as the final musical collaboration between the two greatest songwriters in pop music history.

CHAPTER 14

A MOUSE AND A CONTRACT
How Disney World Became the Backdrop for the Dissolution of the Beatles

Nonstop litigation dogged the Beatles for years, squelching any hope of reconciliation and reunion. From Paul's lawsuit to dissolve their partnership in 1970, through dozens of court cases over the following four years, their legal feuds cost them millions and were sapping the life force out of the four former bandmates.

In late 1974, a small army of lawyers drew up a comprehensive settlement of the Beatles' business issues and scheduled a meeting for December 19 in New York City, where they would gather to sign the papers granting them personal, artistic, and financial freedom. This is the story of how John Lennon skipped the meeting, went to Florida, and visited Disney World, where he finally signed the papers that formally disbanded the Beatles.

"Take off your goddamn shades and get the fuck over here."

George Harrison's frustration with John Lennon had finally pushed the limits of the so-called quiet Beatle. His anger boiled over in a phone call to his onetime bandmate.

It was December 19, 1974, and two of the feuding Beatles, Paul and George, plus a phalanx of lawyers and managers, had gathered at the Plaza Hotel, situated on Fifth Avenue and Central Park in New York City. Ironically, the Plaza had hosted the Beatles on their epochal first visit to America in February 1964, when John, Paul, George, and Ringo famously ran the gauntlet of screaming fans, reporters, and photographers just to enter the landmark hotel.

The scene at the Plaza a decade later, in the dawn of winter 1974, was a stark contrast. No screaming fans crowded the hotel, and no reporters shouted their questions or jockeyed for photos. Paul and Linda brought a movie camera to record the event, but otherwise, no media were on hand for the momentous occasion.

Ten years after their triumphal first visit to the US, dour lawyers and reams of paper arrayed neatly on a large conference room table had replaced the joyous optimism of "I Want to Hold Your Hand" and "She Loves You." This was the designated time and the chosen place for what would be the last act in the years-long drama that had plagued the Beatles since their demise as a functioning band in 1969. Everyone understood that John, Paul, and George were to be physically present at the meeting; Ringo would participate by phone.

One Beatle, however, was missing from this carefully constructed confab. Although John lived within walking distance of the Plaza, he was, thus far, a no-show.

It was no easy feat to get the Beatles together. Visa problems and celebrity schedules were only a few of the formidable challenges to getting the four famous men together in the same room.

George was in New York for shows at Madison Square Garden during his Dark Horse tour, and Paul and Linda had come specifically for the meeting. Ringo had already signed the voluminous papers and would present himself telephonically to verify his assent to the execution of the legal documents.

Given the complex choreography necessary to put the Beatles and their lawyers, managers, and handlers in one place at one time—a logistical challenge not unlike the mobilization of a MASH unit—George's uncontained frustration with John's absence was understandable.

The last time all four Beatles had gathered in a studio was August 20, 1969, when they came together at a mixing session for *Abbey Road* tracks. Their last recording session took place on January 4, 1970, with only three of the four bandmates in attendance, John again being the only absentee. The last time all four Beatles had even been physically together in the same room was during desultory business meetings on September 17, 1969.

Since the death of Brian Epstein in 1967, the Beatles had been adrift without a permanent manager. Paul had fulfilled the role on a de facto basis, rallying the others to the recording studio and even managing to make the *Magical Mystery Tour* film soon after Brian's death. But this approach was nothing more than a temporary fix, and the Beatles began to irrevocably drift apart. As John recalled in a 1973 interview, "Brian just died, and that left us really in the air. We didn't know anything about the business, not one iota about it."

In the business dispute that essentially became the seed of their storied legal and financial troubles, John, George, and Ringo had turned over management of the Beatles' Apple Corps, the company they had formed to manage their affairs, to notorious music industry heavyweight Allen Klein. Wary of Klein's reputation for self-dealing, Paul tried to persuade his dispirited bandmates to steer clear of the thuggish, indelicate Klein, who could not have been more different from the dearly departed Brian Epstein.

The management alternative that Paul put forth was summarily rejected by the other Beatles: his soon-to-be father-in-law, Lee Eastman (who, ironically, had been born with the last name of Epstein), and brother-in-law John Eastman. The sad irony is that Harvard Law School graduate Lee Eastman and his son were eminently qualified entertainment industry lawyers whose savvy would be later confirmed with advice that made Paul a billionaire. But in early 1969, after almost eighteen rudderless months without a manager, the other Beatles were not willing to accept members of Paul's family and their perceived, built-in bias as the group's business managers.

Despite Klein's reputation, the pudgy, abrasive New Jersey native had an uncanny ability to gain the trust of some of the biggest musical acts of the time, both in the US and in Europe. He did this by uncovering millions in unpaid royalties that record companies notoriously hid from unsuspecting musicians. Since royalties were based on record sales, the record companies had concocted some crafty methods of concealing true sales figures from artists and their comparatively naive managers, many of whom were not much older or more experienced than the artists they managed. Klein became a master at conducting what today would be termed "forensic audits" of record company sales figures, digging down deep and dissecting everything from the amount of raw vinyl ordered at record-pressing plants to the number of labels and sleeves printed for singles and albums.

Klein skillfully leveraged record company deception into artist advocacy. However, most of his clients, at least initially, didn't realize that his purported advocacy in opening the record companies' financial spigots also afforded him an opportunity for self-enrichment—at their expense.

Klein's tactics with his clients would be considered predatory today. He would ingratiate himself to new clients by securing advance royalty deals to furnish financially strapped rock stars with up-front boluses of cash, which often became lifelines for coffers depleted by lives of excess. After making his initial down payments on their loyalties, Klein would make his clients lofty promises wrapped in the smooth talk of an East Coast hustler. He would then rob them on the back end by locking up their publishing copyrights and recording masters in perpetuity.

Most young artists were simply outmatched when it came to Klein's business savvy, and they signed contracts without knowing their true contents or consequences. Of course, Klein never suggested that his rock star clients consult with their own attorneys prior to signing the agreements that he and his lawyers had prepared. After all, Klein would have his clients believe *he* was the one looking out for their interests.

Allen Klein (*left*) with John and Yoko, 1969. *Photo: Pictorial Press Ltd. / Alamy*

In 1969, Klein's personal charm and supposed financial wizardry enchanted three of the four Beatles, and, in one of the only key decisions they ever made that was less than unanimous, John, George, and Ringo hired him to manage Apple and them personally. Paul never engaged Klein as his own representative; however, outvoted, he had no choice but to accept him as the manager of Apple and the Beatles. The "all for one and one for all" ethos that had guided the Beatles throughout their career together had dissolved into the cold reality that one-quarter of any four-person partnership could be frozen out of any business decision with which he did not agree.

Life under Allen Klein's management became a joyless affair. Most of the Apple staff—loyalists who had, in some cases, been working with Brian Epstein and the Beatles for years—were unceremoniously handed pink slips in the cold calculus of cost cutting and corporate profitability.

Klein also inserted himself into what was previously a sacrosanct domain open only to the Beatles themselves and George Martin: the music.

Klein had unilaterally brought in Phil Spector to complete the tapes from the *Get Back* sessions, later titled *Let It Be*, and then released the album over Paul's express objections. Spector had altered some of Paul's songs, most famously by his postproduction addition of lush orchestration to "The Long and Winding Road." Paul, in a famous letter to Klein that ended curtly with the words "Don't ever do it again," had unsuccessfully tried to eliminate Spector's musical modifications before the album's release. (Whether Paul was genuinely trying to cut Spector's overdubs is a debatable point, since the letter was dated April 14, 1970, after *Let It Be* was already in pressing, a fact Paul likely knew when he wrote the letter.)

After the Beatles ceased functioning as a working band and transitioned to solo artists, Klein's control over Apple meant that he continued to control issues such as the timing and promotion of their individual album releases. To make matters worse, each Beatle was entitled to share equally in the profits generated by Apple titles. This meant that, for example, Paul's solo work would enrich his estranged bandmates and the manager he despised.

Paul ultimately found his situation of indentured servitude to be a loathsome and untenable asphyxiation of his personal artistic, business, and financial freedom. On advice from the Eastmans, on December 31, 1970, Paul sued his bandmates and childhood friends to dissolve the Beatles' partnership. Although it became easy to paint him in the press as the protagonist of the Beatles' demise, even the other Beatles would ultimately come to appreciate the wisdom of this action.

After nearly a decade of composing some of the most creative, inspiring music in history, the Beatles' magic and legacy were now reduced to a legal writ titled thus:

A declaration that the partnership business carried on by the plaintiff and defendants under the name of The Beatles and Co., and constituted by a deed of partnership dated 19 April 1967 and made between the parties hereto, ought to be dissolved and that accordingly the same be dissolved.

The poetry of "In My Life," "Let It Be," and "A Day in the Life" was now transformed into the bitter, soulless paragraphs of commercial litigation, styled as Case M 6315 of the Chancery Division of the London High Court of Justice:

James Paul McCartney, Plaintiff

v.

John Ono Lennon, George Harrison, Richard Starkey and Apple
Corps, Ltd.

The basis of Paul's lawsuit was fourfold:

(1) The Beatles had long since ceased to perform as a group,

(2) the other Beatles had imposed upon him a wholly unacceptable
manager,

(3) his artistic freedom was subject to undue interference under the
partnership, and

(4) no partnership financial accounts had ever been prepared under
the agreement in effect since 1967.

Although Klein protested that granting Paul's dissolution lawsuit would
create untold tax liabilities, Paul was confident that breaking up the Beatles'
legal partnership was the only avenue available to him to claim his
independence as an artist.

On March 12, 1971, the Rt. Hon. Lord Justice Stamp delivered his
verdict in the case of *McCartney v. Lennon et al.*: a London accountant
would be appointed as the Beatles' official receiver and manage their
assets until such time as the Beatles' legal partnership was dissolved. This
decision effectively ended Allen Klein's management of Apple and
divested him of the authority to continue overseeing the musicians' affairs
and finances. All would now be in the hands of a court-appointed
official—a situation that would present its own difficulties and limitations
over the next four years, tying up much of the cash the Beatles needed
to maintain their lifestyles.

The losing Beatles appealed the judge's ruling but soon abandoned their
effort, perhaps sensing its ultimate futility. Paul had won his case, but the
clouds of uncertainty and dependency continued to hang over their lives.
The judge's ruling extricated Paul and his estranged mates from Allen Klein's
day-to-day control, but the fact that Apple was stuck in receivership continued
to constrain them. Too many issues were still unresolved with the Beatles'
partnership for any of them to achieve true and total freedom.

Allen Klein would remain the manager of John, George, and Ringo
individually until 1973.

Klein's gloss started to wear off first for George after Klein had famously failed to register the August 1971 Concert for Bangladesh as a tax-exempt, charitable organization with the IRS, tying up the concert proceeds and imperiling George's personal finances in the process. Klein's star had similarly faded in John's eyes. By the end of March 1973, John and George made it known that they no longer wanted to be represented by Allen Klein; although not personally dissatisfied with Klein, Ringo went along with the termination precipitated by the other two Beatles.

Finally, Allen Klein was out as manager to Apple and the Beatles. This finale certainly took place under far less tragic circumstances than the end of Brian Epstein's managerial tenure in 1967, but it spawned a new wave of lawsuits between Klein and his three former Beatle clients. This must have, at least in a small way, served as a source of satisfaction for Paul, whom the others finally recognized was right about Klein all along.

The removal of Klein was a necessary first step if there was ever to be a full-fledged Beatles reunion. The Beatles' banishment of this music business brute also paved the way for the global resolution of their vast web of lawsuits and countersuits, which culminated in the December 19, 1974, meeting at the Plaza.

Paul and George, the Eastmans, lawyers and managers for George and Ringo, and Apple caretaker and Beatles childhood friend Neil Aspinall gathered around the huge conference room table, with stacks of paper meticulously arranged for the most anticlimactic closing of all time. Minutes and then hours ticked by as they waited for John to show up.

Although Beatles lore has long held that John's reason for blowing off the Plaza meeting was that "the stars aren't right," the truth was that he remained concerned about the tax implications of a certain clause of the deal, on the basis of his residency in the United States.

May Pang, John's girlfriend during his eighteen-month separation from Yoko, was deputized in the December 19 phone call to tell John's lawyer, Harold Seider, that his client would not be attending the momentous meeting, prompting George's profanity-laced outburst.

The spat over John's no-show put the brakes on a mini reunion planned for later that evening: he was scheduled to join George onstage at his Madison Square Garden concert, as he had done a few weeks earlier at Elton John's famous Thanksgiving show at the Garden (which turned out to be John's final performance before a concert audience). As John recalled:

Somehow or other I was informed that I needn't bother to go to George's show. I was quite relieved in the end, because there wasn't any time for rehearsal, and I didn't want it to be a case of just John jumping up and playing a few chords.

The following day, the pin was placed back in the Beatles' grenade when John met Paul at the Eastmans' law office and then visited with George backstage at his final Garden show of the night. With a truce in place, John, May, and John's son Julian left New York for a Christmas vacation in Florida.

At the time John split New York for Florida, the outstanding business of the unsigned dissolution papers remained unresolved.

Over the course of the next few days, the lawyers addressed John's lingering concerns about expat tax implications, and the mammoth packet of papers was couriered down to the Sunshine State on December 29, 1974. Although John was based in Palm Beach during his vacation, he and May took Julian for an overnight trip to Disney World, which had opened near Orlando in 1971.

John, appropriately dressed for the locale, with May Pang and John's son Julian, in Florida, 1974. *Photo: John Rodgers / Redferns / Getty Images*

John, May, and Julian saw Disney World with the help of a VIP tour guide, who snuck them into the private entrances of the most-popular rides, bypassing the exceptionally long lines that had already become typical of Disney World around the holidays. Despite the large crowds and the rumor that had been making the rounds that day at the Magic Kingdom that a Beatle was on the grounds, John moved about largely unrecognized during his day at Disney.

John later recalled a ride on the famous monorail across the park:

> I heard someone with his back to me say that George Harrison was there today. The guy was leaning on me, and he'd heard that a Beatle was there somewhere. He couldn't see the wood for the trees.

US president Richard Nixon famously proclaiming, "I am not a crook," at Disney World, a little more than a year before John Lennon's visit. *Photo: AP/Shutterstock*

The trio stayed that night at Disney's Polynesian Village Resort, one of the only two hotels on the Disney property at the time, the other being the Contemporary Resort. (Ironically, a year prior, US president Richard Nixon, embroiled in the Watergate scandal, gave a press conference at the Disney Contemporary Resort on November 17, 1973, and uttered what would become one of the most defining statements of his presidency: "People have got to know whether their president is a crook. Well, I'm not a crook." It would mark the beginning of the end for the president, who, evidence would later reveal, had personally used the weight of his office to try [unsuccessfully] to throw John Lennon out of the United States.)

The Apple courier caught up with John at the Polynesian, where he was staying in a ground-floor room in the Samoa longhouse overlooking the Seven Seas Lagoon. After looking over the documents and placing one final call to his lawyer in New York, John was satisfied that both the stars and the tax provisions were properly aligned. He was finally prepared to sign the stack of papers that would, once and for all, end the Beatles' partnership and resolve the web of life-draining business, legal, and financial disputes that had shadowed him and the other Beatles since their breakup.

May Pang later recounted that as he prepared to sign the papers, John "looked wistfully out the window," as if he were "replaying the entire Beatles experience in his mind."

According to May:

> He finally picked up his pen and, in the unlikely backdrop of the Polynesian Village Resort at Disney World, ended the greatest rock-and-roll band in history by simply signing "John Lennon" at the bottom of the page.

A world-changing band that began with the simple meeting of two teenagers at the Woolton village fete in Liverpool on July 6, 1957, now officially ended on December 29, 1974, in a quiet hotel room at Walt Disney World. In the seventeen years, five months, and twenty-three days in between, the Beatles created the most successful and enduring popular music ever made.

POSTSCRIPT

A little more than ten years elapsed between the end of the Beatles as a working band and the irrevocable loss of the first of them from this world. The September 1969 business meetings would turn out to be the last time all four Beatles were ever in the same room at the same time. Although three of them would gather on several occasions in the ensuing years, never again did the four of them congregate at the same place at the same time.

It is hard to imagine that the Beatles realized that such a mundane meeting would be the last time the four of them would be together. "Sometimes," Dr. Seuss once wrote, "you will never know the value of a moment until it becomes a memory."

Although the reasons for the Beatles' breakup have generated a veritable cottage industry of books, articles, and analysis, one factor that surely played an outsized if not determinative role, probably even more so than the much-maligned presence of Yoko Ono, was the entry of Allen Klein into their world.

The decision to hire him was not only a key factor in the ultimate breakup of the band, but his personal retention by three of the Beatles crushed any hope of a reunion in the early 1970s. As John himself said, "The Klein-Eastman situation is what really pushed [the breakup] over the hill."

The early 1970s saw several tantalizing opportunities for the Beatles to reunite, when their physical proximity to one other made the unthinkable possible, but surely the disputes engendered by the presence of Allen Klein in their professional lives prevented that from happening.

The other Beatles would ultimately come to regret their association with Klein, suing him and his companies for fraud, breach of contract, misrepresentation, and a host of other violations of their trust. As John famously said in an interview about the end of his relationship with Klein:

I don't want to go into detail about it, but let's just say that possibly Paul's suspicions were right. Although I hadn't been happy for quite some time with the situation, I didn't want to make any quick moves and I wanted to see if maybe something could work out.

The Rolling Stones also had a long and litigious history with Allen Klein that began with a suit in 1971 and a settlement in 1972, followed by a wave of additional suits over publishing, unpaid royalties, recordings, and other issues.

Klein was convicted of tax crimes in New York in 1971, while Paul's suit in London for dissolution of the Beatles' partnership was pending. Klein was not a party to the dissolution suit, but the fact of his conviction in New York certainly did not escape the judge's notice in London. Klein appealed that conviction, but he was subsequently charged in 1977 with multiple felony counts of tax evasion and ultimately served two months in jail in 1980, a sentence that in no way hurt his established reputation as a tough street fighter. Klein was released from prison a few months before the death of his former client John Lennon.

Allen Klein died in 2009 at the age of seventy-seven, after suffering from diabetes, heart disease, and Alzheimer's for many years. Through his ABKCO company, his estate to this day still owns the rights to all Rolling Stones songs made between 1965 and 1970, the period in which he served as their manager.

One of the dissolution documents signed by John Lennon at Disney World on December 29, 1974, was auctioned by Sotheby's in 2018 and sold for $118,750.

Although the dissolution documents signed by the Beatles in December 1974 ended their musical partnership and resolved the complex web of business entanglements among and between them, it did not completely sever their business interests from one other. Apple Corps continued—and continues to this day—as a going concern to handle the Beatles' extensive and perpetually profitable business affairs.

Disney World bills itself as "the Most Magical Place on Earth." The Beatles brought magic to the world in the 1960s, and their music and legacy have continued to work magic ever since. That their formal partnership should end in a quiet room at Disney World with a solitary signature was a jarring juxtaposition to that magic.

CHAPTER 15

"TRY TO GIVE, AND YOU WILL RECEIVE"

The Heartbreaking Story of a Gentle Giant and His Life of Service to the Beatles

From 1962 through their breakup, a small but fiercely loyal cadre of road managers and personal assistants attended to the Beatles. Perhaps few were as eager to serve them as Mal Evans. "Big Mal," or the "Gentle Giant" as he was sometimes called, stood a burly 6 feet, 3 inches and cut an imposing figure as a bouncer at the Cavern Club, where he first came to the attention of George and then, ultimately, to the attention of the Fab Four.

Present at the Beatles' sides but hidden in their shadows as they conquered the world, Mal unfailingly and without complaint catered to their personal needs, hauled their gear, and set it up for shows around the globe—right through to the rooftop gig in 1969. After the Beatles' breakup, Mal drifted and sought refuge in pills and booze. This is the story of Mal's life of service and the sad, shocking end of one of the Beatles' longest and closest confidants.

"Police officers! Come out with your hands up!" commanded a patrolman to a solitary figure sitting on the bedroom floor of a Los Angeles house on a January night in 1976.

One wonders whether in this moment Mal Evans's mind replayed his decade of past glories at the side of the most popular band and most famous men in the world.

Though they'd met Mal as early as 1961, their friendship began in 1963, when their regular roadie Neil Aspinall was temporarily under the weather, and the Beatles needed someone to take them to gigs and mind their gear. George had become friendly with a particular doorman at the Cavern Club and was impressed by his polite demeanor and hefty frame, which was undoubtedly capable of humping their heavy amps and drums in and out of venues across the north of England. Realizing that their burgeoning schedule necessitated a second full-time roadie in their ranks, the Beatles and their manager offered this genial bloke a full-time job as an assistant road manager.

Malcolm "Mal" Evans entered the Beatles' orbit on a full-time basis on August 11, 1963, as stardom loomed and their schedules became unforgiving. From that day on, Mal became one of the most loyal servants and trusted confidants of the Beatles, privy to the private lives of John, Paul, George, and Ringo from a vantage point that few would ever see.

Mal Evans was born in 1935, in Liverpool, making him five years older than the eldest Beatle, closer to a contemporary of Brian Epstein than of any of the band members. While working for the British Post Office, Mal took on his part-time gig on the Cavern door. His height and build made him an imposing figure by outward appearance, but he was almost universally described as one of the nicest and sweetest people one could meet. He was sometimes referred to as the "Gentle Giant" or "Big Mal."

By this time, Mal was married to a woman named Lily (known as Lil) and had a young son, Gary. He had started working the side job at the Cavern to better support his family. Mal had stopped in to listen to the Beatles play a matinee show on his lunch break, and although he was a big fan of Elvis ("at 6' 3", I'm one of the biggest," he would later say), Mal was instantly drawn to the music and personality of the young Beatles.

Mal first came to the attention of George Harrison, whom he befriended while chatting him up between sets. When the Cavern needed a doorman, it was George who recommended Big Mal to club owner Ray McFall. Mal thus became a regular presence at the venue where the Beatles played more than any other, appearing there nearly three hundred times before their last Cavern show in August 1963, coincidentally right around the time Mal joined them full-time.

Initially Mal served as an assistant roadie to Neil Aspinall, but he eventually assumed the primary roadie role to allow Neil, who had an accounting background and a business mind, to focus on assisting Brian Epstein and attending to the Beatles' personal needs. Together with Neil, Mal would serve by their sides as they toured Europe and ultimately took the United States by storm when Beatlemania descended on America in full throttle in early 1964. Neil and Mal by necessity became master forgers, often signing the Beatles'

Mal Evans tending to Ringo's drum kit in 1964. *Photo: Trinity Mirror / Mirrorpix / Alam*

names to giveaway photos to fulfill the crush of autograph requests (and forever necessitating that generations of memorabilia collectors use great care in discerning fake Beatles' signatures from the real deal).

Mal was present at the Beatles' famed meeting with Elvis in 1965, which he said was one of the biggest thrills of his life. He was, however, mortified when Elvis asked for a guitar pick, and Mal, who nearly always had one in his pocket to fulfill frequent Beatle requests for a "pleck" (or "plectrum," as they were called in the UK), did not have one. Mal forever after kicked himself for not having a pick on hand to loan to Elvis and keep as a souvenir of this most treasured meeting.

When the Beatles stopped touring in the summer of 1966, Mal's role changed, but his place at the side of the Beatles did not. Mal transitioned from roadie to personal assistant as he continued his life of service to the Beatles. John would mutter, "Socks, Mal," and off he would go to buy new socks for a Beatle. He traveled with the Beatles, individually and as a unit, both to keep them company and meet their needs while away from home. Mal traveled with Paul on an African safari and was one of the few members of the Beatles' inner circle to attend Paul's wedding to Linda in 1969, serving as an official witness to the nuptials at the Marylebone Registry Office.

Mal would even figure into some of the songs and albums the Beatles produced over the latter half of their career. Although the origin story of the name "Sgt. Pepper's Lonely Hearts Club Band" has differed over time, many accounts trace it to a conversation between Paul and Mal on an airplane flight and the "salt and pepper" shakers in the first-class cabin. Various accounts suggest that either Paul misheard Mal saying "salt and pepper" as "Sgt. Pepper," or Mal naively asked Paul what the "S" and "P" referred to on the shakers. Regardless of which version is accurate, it seems that Mal figures into the origin story. He would later work with Neil to procure copies of all the photos of the famous faces that appear on the iconic album cover by photographer Peter Blake.

Mal fingered organ notes for a Beatles track in 1965 and sat at one of the four pianos in EMI's Studio Two that simultaneously played a booming E-major chord to unforgettably close "A Day in the Life." Mal had also counted out the twenty-four bars of the track's unfinished middle section, vestiges of which can be heard on the master, upon which the orchestral crescendo that tied together the disparate Lennon and McCartney sections of the song was later added. Most unforgettably, Mal set off the clanging alarm clock at the end of the crescendo, meant as a joke to "wake up" Ringo as a cue. Because the ringing alarm fortuitously coincided with the first lyric of Paul's section ("Woke up, fell out of bed . . .") and because of the near impossibility of removing it from the master tape, the whimsical clanging clock was retained in the final master.

Mal also played bit parts in most of the Beatles' movies, from a brief appearance in *A Hard Day's Night* to his more memorable turn as a wayward swimmer in *Help!* and as a magician in *Magical Mystery Tour*. He also figured in scenes in *Let It Be*, moving equipment and hammering the anvil during rehearsals of "Maxwell's Silver Hammer" (although Ringo would have the honors for the studio version).

According to portions of Mal's diary, which turned up in later years, Mal also had a hand in writing lyrics for portions of Beatles compositions. His diary entries also suggest that he was assured that he would receive songwriting credit—and thus royalties—for his efforts, although neither the credit nor the compensation ever came to pass. This was a crushing but quiet disappointment on the part of the Gentle Giant, who was paid less than £40 per week during most of his years with the Beatles. He wrote in his diary how much the anticipated royalty payments would ease the burdens on him and his family, which grew by one with the birth of his daughter, Julie, in 1966. Alas, Mal never profited from his purported lyrical contributions.

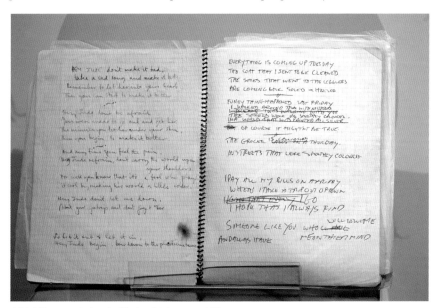

A Mal Evans notebook. *Photo: PA Images / Alamy*

Mal's diaries reveal troubling inner turmoil behind his outward displays of geniality. As George would say years later in *Anthology* interviews, Mal "was one of those people who loved what he was doing and didn't have any problems about service" to others. Yet, in his diaries, Mal admitted that he felt undervalued by the Beatles, both financially and as a person. In one of the most poignant passages, Mal wrote

> I feel very hurt and sad inside—only big boys don't cry. Why I should feel hurt and reason for writing this is ego—I thought I was different from other people in my relationship with the Beatles[,] and being loved by them and treated so nice, I felt like one of the family. Seems I fetch and carry—I always tell myself—look, everybody wants to take from, be satisfied, try to give and you will receive. After all this time I have about £70 to my name but was content and happy. Loving them as I do, nothing is too much trouble, because I want to serve them.

"Try to give and you will receive." What an incredibly poignant and insightful sentiment. It seems to sum up the life of quiet service lived by this intriguing and ultimately tragic figure so central to the Beatles' story.

Although Mal was not generously paid or sufficiently appreciated, the opportunity to serve such creative, vibrant, and admired men as the Beatles apparently gave him an inner fulfillment that neither money nor adulation could buy. Nevertheless, knowing the tragedy that ultimately befell him makes Mal's diary entries so much more touching and painful when reading them with the benefit of hindsight.

After Apple Corps became the Beatles' umbrella entity for their varied business interests, Mal became an Apple employee. And like other Apple employees, Mal and his portfolio of freewheeling Beatle-indulging duties came under the cost-cutting eye of Allen Klein. After asserting that Mal and others were "living like kings" on Apple's dime, Klein fired him in 1969. Shortly after, he was rehired after personal intervention by three of the Beatles themselves.

While at Apple, in addition to continuing in his role as personal assistant to the Beatles, Mal styled himself as a talent scout and record producer. Most notably, Mal is credited with "discovering" the Iveys—later known as Badfinger—an early and quite successful Apple Records signing. The group had also crossed the radar of Peter Asher, Apple's A&R (artists and repertoire) man and future Grammy-winning producer, but Mal undoubtedly played a role in the profitable union between Badfinger and Apple.

By 1973, Mal relocated to Los Angeles to remain in the orbit of the solo Beatles who'd relocated there, most notoriously John during his "lost weekend." Indeed, Mal became one of the members of the West Coast troupe of self-destructive partiers that included Harry Nilsson, John, May Pang, Keith Moon, Ringo, and other notable purveyors of rock excess.

When Mal decamped to L.A. he left his wife, Lil, in the process and took up with Fran Hughes, a woman he had met at the Record Plant. Evidence suggests that a convergence of events, including his inability to

●   ● Page 1, Copy *5*

OFFICER-INVOLVED SHOOTING REPORT

DR 76-430 212
245 P.C. SUSPECT
EVANS, Malcolm (DECEASED)
Male Caucasian, 40

INVOLVED OFFICERS:

D. D. KREMPA, 14918, 7Z24
R. E. BRANNON, 15897, 7A51

DATE AND TIME OF SHOOTING: January 4, 1976, 2100 hours

LOCATION OF SHOOTING: ▇ West 4th Street

AREA OF OCCURRENCE: Wilshire Area
R/D 703

OFFICER-INVOLVED SHOOTING TEAM: INV. III R. L. CALKINS, 7287
INV. II J. E. COINER, 10482

CONFIDENTIAL

THIS REPORT IS FOR THE CONFIDENTIAL USE OF THE CITY ATTORNEY

TO: BURT PINES, CITY ATTORNEY

Sir:

CHRONOLOGICAL NARRATIVE

On Sunday, 1-4-76, at approximately 2015 hours, ▇▇▇▇ received a telephone call from a friend, ▇▇▇▇. She told ▇▇▇▇ that ▇▇▇▇, Malcolm Evans, had taken nine or ten Valium pills and threatened suicide. She said he was despondent and she was worried. ▇▇▇▇ advised her to call a doctor and then terminated the phone conversation.

At approximately 2030 hours, he received another call from ▇▇▇▇. She stated that Evans wanted ▇▇▇▇ to come to their residence and witness a will. ▇▇▇▇ drove to the ▇▇▇▇ residence at ▇▇▇▇, arriving at approximately 2045 hours. He observed Evans writing on stationery in the downstairs living room.

▇▇▇▇ persuaded Evans, in ▇▇▇▇ presence, to go upstairs to their bedroom. ▇▇▇▇ accompanied Evans to the front (north) bedroom of the two-story apartment. Upon entering the bedroom, Evans picked up a .30-.30 lever-action rifle. ▇▇▇▇ became apprehensive and left the room and returned downstairs. He related his observation to ▇▇▇▇ who immediately went to the bedroom. She observed Evans with the rifle and informed him that she was going downstairs and call the police. He yelled, "Go ahead and call the police."

The LAPD police report of the January 4, 1976, incident involving Mal Evans. *Photo: LAPD archives*

become a "true" record producer, estrangement from his wife and kids (Lil had asked him for a divorce in December 1975), and the pressures of delivering a promised memoir (*Living the Beatles Legend*, as it was to be called), caused Mal to drift. He was known to use alcohol and pills in this period.

These events and pressures came to a head on the night of Sunday, January 4, 1976 (although, inexplicably, much of the documentation about Mal on the internet states that the date was January 5 or 6). There are several differing published accounts of what happened that night; however, the following facts, unless otherwise noted, are taken directly from the LAPD police report:

At approximately 8:15 p.m., Mal's girlfriend, Fran Hughes, called a man named John Hoernle, who was helping Mal with photos for his Beatles memoir, and asked him to come to their rented house at 8122 W. 4th Street in the Wilshire area of L.A. Hughes told Hoernle that Mal had taken nine or ten Valium pills and threatened suicide. Hoernle advised Hughes to call a doctor. About fifteen minutes later, she called Hoernle again, this time telling him that Mal wanted him to come to the house and witness a will. Hoernle arrived at the residence at approximately 8:45 p.m.

Upon arrival at the house, with Hughes looking on, Hoernle persuaded Mal to go upstairs, with Hoernle accompanying him. Once there, Mal picked up what the police report indicates was a .30-.30 lever-action rifle. Most internet accounts refer to the weapon as an "air gun" that was "mistaken" by the police as a "real" weapon, but the police report makes no mention of the rifle being an air gun. In fact, the LAPD analysis of the weapon also concluded that the rifle was chambered with one live round of ammunition and three more rounds in the magazine, one of which was a hollow-point bullet, a variety of ammunition known to be more lethal than a standard round. The police report notes that a .22-caliber pistol was also found in Mal's bedroom.

Hoernle became apprehensive when Mal displayed the rifle, and retreated downstairs. He related to Hughes his observation about Mal with the rifle, and she went upstairs and observed the same scene. At that point, she told Mal that she was going to go downstairs to call the police.

"Go ahead and call the police," Mal is alleged to have said in reply, according to the LAPD report.

Around that time, Hughes called LAPD and informed them that Mal was making suicidal statements, had taken pills, and had a rifle.

By the time Fran Hughes hung up the phone, the wheels of tragedy were set into motion.

Within two minutes, LAPD officers Krempa and Herman arrived in an LAPD patrol car. Hughes met them in front of the residence, telling the officers that Mal was despondent, had taken Valium, had a rifle (again, there was no mention that the weapon was an "air rifle"), and had "flipped out." Hughes's four-year-old daughter was in the back bedroom, and she cautioned the officers to be mindful of the child. The officers entered the house, Krempa armed with a shotgun and Herman with his service revolver, which was drawn as they made their way upstairs.

Another LAPD patrol unit arrived at this time, with Officers Brannon and Simonsen, also brandishing their unholstered .38-caliber service revolvers.

"Police officers! Come out with your hands up!" Officers Herman and Krempa both shouted. The time was right around 9:00 p.m.

Officer Krempa kicked open the closed door to Mal's bedroom right as fellow officers Brannon and Simonsen made it to the stop of the stairs.

When the door to the bedroom flung open, the officers got their first look at Big Mal Evans.

They knew nothing of Mal's gentle disposition, that he was a nearly universally loved member of the Beatles' inner circle, or that he had two young children of his own. They merely observed a large man, seated on the floor with his legs out in front of him, holding in his hands a lever-action rifle, pointed upward at a 30-degree angle.

The police report refers to the officers again shouting commands for Mal to "drop the gun."

According to the report, Mal responded, "No, blow my head off."

The report goes on to allege that Mal then raised the rifle to his shoulder "as if to fire." The officers reported hearing a metallic "click," as if the rifle were being cocked.

Mal Evans pointing a prop gun on the set of the movie *Blindman*, July 14, 1971, with Ringo looking on. *Photo: Jack Kay / Daily Express / Getty Images*

The fate of the forty-year-old Gentle Giant was now sealed.

Officer Krempa rapidly fired five rounds from his service revolver. Officer Brannon fired one round.

Mal sustained four gunshots. One, to his chest, was almost instantly fatal.

An ambulance was already at the scene, standing by because of the nature of the call as a potential suicide. They could provide no life-sustaining treatment, and Mal Evans was pronounced dead in the second-floor bedroom of his rented L.A. house around 9:00 p.m. on January 4, 1976.

In addition to the two weapons, also recovered as evidence at the house were five pages of stationery on which Mal had written "nearly illegible notes" that "could be construed as a will or a suicide note."

The LAPD report, to the extent that it is an accurate record of what really happened, paints a picture of a phenomenon that is now known as "suicide by cop"; that is, a person lacking the will to commit suicide deliberately puts himself into a provocative or threatening position with the police that leaves them no choice but to shoot.

Many published accounts of Mal's death allege that the police mistook an air gun for a rifle, but the LAPD report reads that there were not one, but two, real guns in the house, one of which, chambered with deadly ammunition, was pointed at the police.

Measured by today's standards, one might perceive this incident as a tragic failure of the mental health system and the prioritization of law enforcement over necessary psychological or substance abuse treatment and intervention. But Mal Evans's fate was sealed the moment he pointed a rifle, or anything that even *looked* like a rifle, in the direction of police officers. Even if it turned out that the rifle *was* an air rifle, the shooting would still have unquestionably been deemed justified under the standards of the time, or likely even under the standards of today.

What is beyond dispute is that the story of the Gentle Giant is one of the saddest chapters in Beatles history. A bear of a man who loyally and uncomplainingly served—and loved—the Beatles, Mal felt undervalued and, at times, unappreciated by his famous employers. Sadly, nothing that happened in his life after the Beatles could possibly measure up to the excitement of his years in the rarefied air of their inner circle.

"Try to give and you will receive," Mal had written in a dark moment of painful reflection, as if to remind himself that there was honor and value in his life of service. Mal lived at the edges of stardom, fame, and fortune, yet he was never able to grab a piece of that brass ring for himself, despite its tantalizing proximity.

Mal would not, of course, be the only member of the Beatles' circle to die by gunfire at the age of forty under shocking and tragic circumstances. While the murder of John Lennon made worldwide headlines, the death of Mal Evans was little noted.

Even in death, Big Mal stood in the shadows of the Beatles.

Mal Evans, *far left*, literally standing in the shadow of the Beatles. *Photo: Trinity Mirror / Mirrorpix / Alamy*

POSTSCRIPT

In one of the more tragic coincidences further connecting Mal's death with the murder of John Lennon, Cynthia Lennon in her book *John* tells a remarkable story about the night her former husband was killed.

Cynthia happened to be visiting with Maureen "Mo" Starkey, Ringo's ex-wife, on the evening of December 8, 1980. While the two ex-Beatle wives and old friends downed a couple of bottles of wine and reminisced, the subject of Mal Evans's death came up. Remembering Mal fondly as a "faithful friend" of the Beatles who had been "lost" after the band's breakup, they puzzled over how someone so gentle, whom they believed could no more have shot a person than flown to the moon, could have met such a violent end.

"To us," Cynthia wrote, "the idea of being shot was almost unimaginable— how could it have happened to such a good friend?"

After Cynthia had gone to sleep, she was awakened by Mo's screams, and Mo burst into her room: "Cyn, John's been shot. Ringo's on the phone— he wants to talk to you."

The confluence of John's death on a night that two former Beatles' wives commiserated over the tragic death of Mal Evans four years earlier is one of the little-known coincidences of these serial tragedies, one of which reverberated within a small circle of friends and family, and the other of which shook the world.

In the internal review of the police response to Mal's shooting, the LAPD concluded that remedial instruction for the involved officers was necessary. Remediation was not meant to discipline them for any misconduct in their decision to shoot Mal. Rather, the officers were counseled that they "should have taken more time to assess the situation properly," and that their decision to enter the house under the circumstances "placed the officers in a position of disadvantage and could have resulted in an officer being killed or seriously injured."

The LAPD review report notes that the officers concurred with these findings and "gained insight and knowledge not here-to-fore possessed," and that they received the department's counseling with "positive attitudes." Mal's shooting was found to be a justifiable homicide.

Mal's body was cremated on January 7, 1976. None of the Beatles attended his funeral. Harry Nilsson retrieved Mal's ashes and sent them back to his family in England by mail, although the postal service misplaced the parcel. John Lennon, whose sense of humor was known to veer into the morbid, was quoted as having remarked, "They should look in the dead-letter file." The package with Mal's mortal remains was ultimately delivered to his family.

Owing to his years in the Beatles' inner circle, Mal Evans reportedly owned a collection of items and documents that would undoubtedly be worth a modest fortune. It has been alleged that Mal had a trunkful of notebooks, lyrics, and other valuable memorabilia, and the elusive case purportedly turned up in a few places around the world. These claims were debunked after closer inspection.

A few pieces of Mal's authenticated Beatles memorabilia have surfaced over the years. None other than Yoko Ono was instrumental in locating these materials when they were retrieved from a publisher's basement in New York.

Mal's estate sold John Lennon's handwritten lyrics to "A Day in the Life" in 1992 for almost $80,000. Paul stepped in to block Lily Evans's attempt to sell the handwritten lyrics to "With a Little Help from My Friends," claiming that Mal was keeping the lyrics as one of his job duties and that they properly belonged to the writers (one wonders what Paul's motivation could have been in preventing the widowed Mrs. Evans from obtaining some recompense for her late husband's years of faithful service). In 1998, one of Mal's notebooks containing draft lyrics for "Hey Jude" and "Sgt. Pepper's Lonely Hearts Club Band" sold for over $150,000.

Neither the complete diary of Mal Evans nor the manuscript for *Living the Beatles Legend* has been made public. Only portions of his diary have surfaced in the media. It is easy to imagine that in these documents Mal wrote invaluable, first-person perspectives on life in the Beatles' inner circle throughout their career. But, knowing the quiet life of respectful and discreet service Mal rendered over the years, one can also imagine that Mal omitted the most-salacious and potentially embarrassing details—loyally serving his beloved Beatles until the very end.

CHAPTER 16

THE APPLE THAT BIT BACK
How Big Tech Swallowed the Beatles' Utopian Vision

After the death of Brian Epstein in August 1967, the Beatles remained musically inventive and lyrically creative, but they twisted in the wind when it came to business affairs. The Beatles launched Apple Corps, conceived as a tax haven, as a utopian incubator of musical, film, and artistic talent, with ill-fated forays into retail and the nascent field of consumer electronics.

This is the story of how the Beatles' vision of an altruistic commercial empire crash-landed under the weight of its own largesse. It is also the story of how serial legal battles with a tech startup saw an eventual David and Goliath role reversal and how a business behemoth swallowed the Beatles' corporate identity.

The Beatles faced a possible £2–3 million tax liability as the curtain fell on a tumultuous 1967. Brian Epstein died in August, and the Beatles lost their single, central source of advice and accountability for their business and financial affairs. Now, a web of lawyers, accountants, and advisors began to step in to try to fill the void.

The Beatles' response was to adopt a tax-avoidance strategy that made the four of them employees of a new corporation instead of four individuals deriving income from their partnership. They adopted the name Apple Corps, a pun on "apple core." It would serve their business interests and give the tax man a smaller bite. But the Beatles imagined their new enterprise as something more. At the outset, at least, they saw Apple Corps as an outlet for their utopian dreams of collective capitalism and a positive force for producing new art, films, and music.

"We're in business. We find ourselves in business," Paul told journalist (and traveling companion from the first two US tours) Larry Kane in 1968. The nascent idea of corporate benevolence not quite fully formed in his mind, Paul added, "But all the profits won't go into our pockets. They'll go to help people—but not like a charity."

Even less farsighted about Apple's role was the dreadfully nearsighted John Lennon, who said of the company as they took their first steps off an uncertain corporate precipice, "It's like a top; we set it going and hope for the best."

From these hazy and unformed visions, the Beatles' intentions for Apple Corps can perhaps best be summarized this way: they wanted to bring the sensibilities of artists, versus the cold calculations of businessmen, to the decisions about what music they would produce and what films they would make. Such distributive notions of artistic egalitarianism might have played better in today's digital age, when the reproduction and distribution of recorded content present fewer barriers to entry and less forbidding costs. But in the late 1960s, films and music required physical media for distribution, sales, and consumption, and the steep costs of market entry meant that gatekeepers and decision makers would still have to play a crucial role. No amount of Beatles earnestness could erase the unavoidable costs of marketing and distributing the art of anyone who asked.

Peter Asher, who became Apple Records' A&R man, and later a Grammy-winning producer, expressed it more charitably: "I think the only plan for Apple was for it to be good music—and ideally music that maybe wasn't getting an opportunity to be heard other places. It really was a case of them having this extraordinary power and influence and using it pretty wisely."

Magic Alex (*right*) with John and Yoko in Greece, November 1969. *Photo: Bettman / Getty Images*

Apple Corps became a conglomerate instead of simply a company. A web of entities, including, most prominently, Apple Records, along with Apple Electronics, Apple Films, Zapple, and others, became vehicles both for serious art and Beatles vanity projects. Apple Electronics was headed by Alexis Mardas, a charismatic charlatan known as "Magic Alex." Most of his inventions, including electrified, color-changing car paint and a force field emitter that would protect the Beatles from overzealous fans, never materialized or failed outright. He did, however, have a particular aptitude for making the Beatles' money disappear.

In his quest to set up a state-of-the-art recording studio in the basement of the Apple building on Savile Row in London, Magic Alex neglected to insulate against the noise of the building's heating system, causing an audible whir of electric fans in the studio. He inexplicably wired in eight separate speakers for an eight-channel mixing board and promised the Beatles seventy-two-track recording capabilities, a virtual impossibility given the technological limitations of the era.

So useless was the Apple studio that the Beatles were forced to borrow a mobile recording unit from EMI to record there in 1969.

Apple Films fared better than Apple Electronics. Releases included *Magical Mystery Tour* (which was panned by critics after its black-and-white airing on Boxing Day in 1967), *Let It Be*, and *The Concert for Bangladesh*, the latter being the film version of the world's first major charity rock concert, almost two decades before Live Aid. (Of note, *Let It Be* received a reboot in late 2021 as a three-part documentary event retitled *Get Back*, which aired on Disney+. The new film accomplished nothing less than a recast of our collective view of the *Let It Be* sessions as a dispirited and disintegrating band into a more positive, upbeat, and creative swan song.)

Another early and ultimately short-lived side venture was the Apple Boutique, a retail store in London that sold clothing, music, incense, and an array of other proto-1960s staples. Originally managed by Pete Shotton, John Lennon's school friend and a former member of the Quarrymen, the boutique closed less than eight months after its auspicious launch, after it lost money hand over fist through pilfered inventory and poor executive leadership. The Beatles liquidated the store's remaining merchandise by giving it away to the public (one item per person) after cherry-picking the stock themselves in the days prior to the final giveaways.

Despite these diversified holdings and some ill-fated ventures, Apple was, at its core (pardon the pun), a music company. Apple Records was the central, most consequential, and most enduring element of the Beatles' business conglomerate. Among its more notable and profitable signings were James Taylor, Mary Hopkin, Billy Preston, and the Iveys, who were later rechristened Badfinger.

Although the recorded work of the Beatles was still subject to their contract with EMI (which would continue to own Beatles masters), Apple Records and EMI entered into a distribution deal (itself the subject of litigation in later years), whereby EMI would distribute Apple Records, including through Capitol Records in the US. The "White Album" (officially, *The Beatles*), *Yellow Submarine*, *Abbey Road*, and *Let It Be* all were Apple titles.

Apple also issued the Beatles' solo records, although by 1975 each member of the group had abandoned their own label and signed deals with other record companies.

In those days, Apple Corps had a well-deserved reputation for hemorrhaging money in countless creative ways. Employees helped themselves to boutique merchandise and had frequent "meetings" at extravagant eateries, where the finest wines flowed freely. The profligate spending of Magic Alex certainly contributed to the bleeding coffers.

Neil Aspinall, *top right*, with the Beatles in the heady days of 1964. *Photo: Hulton Archives / Pace/ Stringer / Getty Images*

So well known was the spendthrift culture of Apple Corps that the 1978 Beatles satire film *All You Need Is Cash*, featuring the fictional Rutles, included a memorable scene in which a variety of interlopers pilfered virtually everything but the bricks on the Rutle Corps building. Like pirates, they carried their booty out the front door in plain sight. The pièce de résistance was the thievery of the very microphone that the fictional correspondent, played by none other than George Harrison in a wonderfully self-effacing cameo, was using to narrate the scene as it unfolded.

Although Klein wielded the ax at Apple and cut off many longtime Beatles' friends and loyalists from the company, one employee was given special protection from the purge—Neil Aspinall. Over the years, Neil served as the Beatles' original road manager and later as a personal assistant when their touring years ended. At Apple, Neil bided his time during the Klein years. However, following the firing of the once-invincible Klein in 1973, Neil officially rose to the position of Apple's chief executive.

The role of Apple Corps' CEO must have been one of the toughest jobs in the world during the years immediately following the Beatles' breakup. The position required a delicate balancing of interests and egos, compelling Neil to be a wholly honest broker in maintaining the confidence of the four most famous—and often feuding—men in the world.

One area in which Neil and the Beatles constantly found common ground was the steadfast protection of their legacy and image. Neil was a relentless guardian of the Beatles' empire, consistently declining licensing requests to use their music for commercial ventures and, notably, becoming "Mr. No" when it came to the digitization of the Beatles' catalog. Other than overseeing the release of their music on compact discs, Neil, on his bosses' behalf, consistently rebuffed overtures to include the Beatles' music on the newly emerging music streaming and downloading services. In this realm, Apple Computer's iTunes was emerging as the most formidable competitor in the market.

One of Neil's signature accomplishments resulted in the most carefully curated presentation of the Beatles' legacy in their postbreakup years: *The Beatles Anthology* project in the 1990s. This offering consisted of a book and a three-episode documentary released in the United States in 1995, which later became an eight-VHS set in 1996 and an eight-DVD set in 2003. Originally conceived as *The Long and Winding Road*, the project was rechristened with the neutral *Anthology* moniker to avoid the appearance of a preference for Paul and his composition from the *Let It Be* album.

While Neil Aspinall settled in at the helm of Apple Corps, two young entrepreneurs working out of a California garage intent on making personal

From left, George Martin, Jeff Lynne, and Neil Aspinall at the launch of *The Beatles Anthology* in 1995. *Photo: Ilpo Musto / Shutterstock*

computers user-friendly launched Apple Computer, Inc., in 1976. Although cofounders Steve Jobs and Steve Wozniak have been quoted and misquoted over the decades about the inspiration for their company's name, at times suggesting it was inspired by Jobs's fruit-based diet or that "Apple" came before "Atari" in telephone listings, Jobs made no secret of the fact that the Beatles were an inspiration. In fact, it was suggested and even hinted at by Jobs himself that the name of his company was directly influenced by Apple Corps.

In 2003, Jobs told *60 Minutes* this:

> My model for business is the Beatles. They were four guys who kept each other's kind of negative tendencies in check. They balanced each other, and the total was greater than the sum of the parts. That's how I see business: Great things in business are never done by one person. They're done by a team of people.

At the dawn of Apple Computer, there was little intersection between PCs, such as the Apple I and Apple II, and the music business. Before sound cards, before MIDI (musical instrument device interface), and long before the iPod and iTunes, music remained almost exclusively a physical medium—records, eight-track tapes, and audiotapes. The only way to hear music wirelessly was through your conventional terrestrial radio. Digital music remained a long way off.

Even though music and computers weren't yet operating in each other's lanes, Apple Corps sued Apple Computer in 1978 for trademark infringement. The guns of this initial salvo fell silent a few years later in a 1981 settlement agreement and a payment by the Jobs-Wozniak camp to the Beatles. The amount was undisclosed at the time, but it was later revealed to be $80,000 (over $260,000 in 2023 dollars).

Although the 1981 settlement agreement was confidential and did not constitute one of the public court filings, it was widely reported that its cornerstone was that Apple Computer would not enter the music business, and Apple Corps would not enter the computer business.

Oh how those lines would blur in the coming years.

In 1986 Apple Computer added MIDI capabilities to its Apple IIGS and then to other models. This meant that, for the first time, its products could render digital music. Apple Corps again filed suit in 1989, this time alleging a violation of the 1981 settlement agreement.

This second round of inter-Apple litigation wrapped up in 1991, with a new settlement agreement and another payment from Apple Computer to Apple Corps. This time, the settlement amount was a reported to be $26.5 million (a little over $57 million in 2023 dollars).

The 1991 settlement would become the centerpiece of yet another round of litigation. Although commentators have widely reported that the original settlement agreement mandated that Apple Computer "stay out of the music business," the real provisions were much more nuanced. In reality, the 1991 settlement agreement represented a clearer vision of the possibilities of digital music distribution than was possible at the time of the earlier settlement. The agreement essentially treated the Apple Corps domain as physical media—such as CDs, records, and tapes—thus preserving the Apple Computer domain in the delivery of digital content and the devices that could translate it into music.

At the time, the 1991 settlement was perceived and reported as a win for Apple Corps over Apple Computer. In reality, it was a contributing factor in Apple Computer ultimately becoming the most valuable company in the world. It also set the stage for another, even-higher-stakes intramural fruit lawsuit, one that would have a drastically different outcome.

In April 2003, Apple Computer launched the iTunes Store, the game-changing digital music-downloading service that sold individual songs for ninety-nine cents apiece, which could be played on the soon-to-be-ubiquitous iPod. The Apple Computer logo, the original source of the Beatles' copyright infringement claims, of course featured prominently on the iTunes branding and marketing.

It did not take long for Apple Corps' lawyers to once again deploy to the legal battlefields of the London High Court. By September 2003, the Beatles' company again sued Apple Computer, this time for alleged violation of the terms of the 1991 settlement agreement. However, legal and music industry experts this time determined that the tables had turned; the distribution of digital music—and the narrow domain of physical media reserved to Apple Corps—would favor Apple Computer.

This time, the case went to trial instead of ending in an out-of-court settlement. The stakes now were simply too high for the parties to come to any financially workable agreement. High Court Justice Edward Mann handed down his ruling on May 8, 2006, switching the opponents' positions in the battle of the Apples.

Persuaded by the much more meticulously crafted and farsighted 1991 settlement agreement, which allowed Apple Computer to use its trademarks on software (such as iTunes) and hardware that could play music (such as the iPod), the court ruled that Apple Computer's use of the disputed trademarks was within its rights as set forth in the earlier agreement. Not only would Apple Computer not be required to pay royalties to Apple Corps, but Apple Corps would be required to pay an estimated £2 million in legal fees to Apple Computer.

Neil Aspinall told the media that Apple Corps believed the trial judge "reached the wrong conclusion," and would appeal the judgment. While the appeal was pending in 2007, Apple Computer, newly rebranded simply as Apple, Inc., and Apple Corps entered into yet another settlement agreement. This time, the agreement reflected the role reversal and relative change in power and bargaining position of the two companies.

Apple Computer's market value hit $100 billion in 2007, meaning that Jobs, Wozniak, and company could afford to buy Apple Corps outright and *still* have almost $100 billion left over. The value of Apple Corps was merely a rounding error on Apple Computer's books.

In perhaps the most symbolic nail ever pounded into the 1960s coffin, all "Apple" trademarks were transferred to Apple Computer, and the Apple Corps logo and certain other intellectual property were licensed back to Apple Corps by the tech giant. As with most such settlements, the actual agreement was confidential and did not become part of the public record, but reports at the time indicated that Apple Computer purchased all rights to the Apple Corps trademarks for $500 million, or about half of 1 percent— that's 0.5 percent for those who benefit from seeing it numerically—of the tech company's value at that time.

The Beatles started Apple Corps on the advice of accountants and advisors who were intent on helping them reduce their tax liabilities. The Beatles envisioned their company, born of business necessity, as a sort of utopian incubator of the arts—the antidote to corporate-run record companies and publishers. A collective run by artists for artists. A way to allow others to realize the dreams that the Beatles themselves had realized in spades.

The fact that the Beatles continue to use their iconic Apple Corps logo only with the permission of one of the biggest tech companies on the planet is a digital-age coda to a distinctly 1960s saga of peace, love, and music.

Steve Jobs proclaiming the availability of the Beatles' music on iTunes, 2010. *Photo: Paul Sakuma / AP / Shutterstock*

POSTSCRIPT

With the 2007 settlement behind them and facing the realization that iTunes was pointing the way toward the digital and online future of the music business, Apple Corps finally relented in November 2010, just in time for the run-up to Christmas, and consented to the Beatles' music appearing on iTunes. A long, winding, and litigious road finally brought the most popular music of all time to the most popular music distribution platform of the age.

Before launching the Beatles' music on iTunes, however, Apple Corps extracted more revenue for itself out of the digitalization of the Beatles' music. The remastered Beatles catalog was issued on CD in the spring of 2009 and enriched Apple Corps yet again, selling more than 2.25 million units worldwide before the end of the year—thirty-nine years after the band had broken up.

An ebullient Paul McCartney, joined by Ringo Starr, appearing at the launch of *The Beatles: Rock Band*, June 1, 2009. *Photo: Damian Dovarganes / AP / Shutterstock*

The Beatles-iTunes collaboration also followed the launch of *The Beatles: Rock Band* video game in September 2009. Although the sales figures were labeled as "disappointing" by tech industry watchers (moving 1.7 million units between September and December 2009) for this cleverly packaged offering—complete with an electronic "drum set," microphone, and Beatle-shaped plastic guitars outfitted with game controllers—it marked the pinnacle of an innovative year that saw the Beatles fully embracing the digital age. Apple Corps was now in the digital business, and Apple Computer was king of the music business. Times had indeed changed.

A truly fab byproduct of the launch of the *Rock Band* game was the separation and isolation of basic instrument tracks to some of the Beatles' best-known recordings. In fact, a search of YouTube will allow listeners to hear bass, guitar, and drum tracks in splendid isolation. These tracks have proven to be invaluable to countless musicians who strive to reproduce every note and nuance of the Fab Four's studio recordings. It is a bit like finding one of Michelangelo's paintbrush bristles on the ceiling of the Sistine Chapel.

However, it would take a change in Apple Corps' leadership before the Beatles were able to fully embrace the digital age and monetize some of its riches. After serving the Beatles for almost fifty years in every capacity, from lowly roadie to CEO of their business empire, Neil Aspinall retired in 2007, shortly after resolution of the last round of Apple-Apple litigation, in which the Beatles' Apple trademarks were transferred to Apple Computer.

Whether Neil's departure was a forced retirement, a voluntary one, or an act of protest remains a source of speculation, but the saddest postscript is that barely over a year after the final Apple settlement agreement was signed, Neil died of lung cancer on March 24, 2008. Stella McCartney attended the funeral on her father's behalf, joined by Barbara Bach (Ringo's wife), Yoko Ono, and Pete Best. It was later revealed that prior to his diagnosis, Neil had postretirement plans as a filmmaker and even to produce a memoir—one of the most revealing looks inside the Beatles' bubble to have never been written. A veritable treasure trove of Beatles history was lost forever with the passing of their longest-serving and most loyal lieutenant.

As of 2023, Apple, Inc., has a market capitalization of nearly 2.6 *trillion* dollars, making it, at times, the most valuable company in the world, depending on the daily markets, and consistently in the top five of companies by value worldwide. Cofounder Steve Jobs, who worshipped the Beatles and was said to have been personally saddened over the years of litigation against his heroes, died at the age of fifty-six in 2011 with a net worth of over $10 billion. Jobs reportedly chose alternative therapies and supplements to treat his pancreatic cancer over traditional medical treatment that experts determined could have prolonged his life. Cofounder Steve Wozniak is, as of 2023, active as a philanthropist.

Apple Corps continues as a vital company to this day, albeit with a licensed logo, the intellectual property of Apple Computer. Apple Corps is currently run by CEO Jeff Jones, and by some reports grossing over £50 million annually, which can spike in years that involve large commercial projects (such as the release of the *Get Back* film in 2021, or the *Revolver* reissue in 2022).

The four owners of Apple Corps in 2023 are James Paul McCartney, Richard Starkey, and the estates of John Lennon and George Harrison.

AFTERWORD

Mythology is a veneer that can be sandblasted only with truth.

The Beatles' creative and commercial accomplishments will likely never be equaled. They've earned their place in the pantheon of history's artistic greats.

Unlike many other bands, the Beatles never reunited after breaking up. The world was left wanting more, right up to the moment a reunion became impossible on the night of December 8, 1980, on a bloody tiled floor of a vestibule in the Dakota Building in New York City.

The veneer of mythology around the Beatles hardened after their irretrievable breakup in 1970. Yet, chipping away at the Beatles' veneer reveals something elemental underneath: their music, lyrics, wit, style, presence, and humor were the real deal. It's not the myth of the Beatles that endures: it's the music.

The Beatles don't need to rely upon mythology. The truth is more than enough. I hope you've enjoyed *Fab but True* and our exploration of how the Beatles' truths are even better than their myth.

BIBLIOGRAPHY

Aldredge, Trip. "Come Together: John Lennon and Morris Levy." *Trip Aldredge's Music and Law Blog*, October 2, 2019.

Babiuk, Andy. *The Beatles Gear—All the Fab Four's Instruments from the Stage to Studio—the Ultimate Edition*. London: Backbeat Books, 2015.

Beatles, The. *Anthology*. San Francisco: Chronicle Books, 2000.

Beatles, The. *The Story of Apple Records Part One*. Video file. December 2, 2010. https://www.youtube.com/watch?v=spRcoGLqj2s.

"The Beatles Career Was Kick Started . . . by a Bet on a Winning Horse!" *The Track Philosopher*, July 21, 2019. https://www.thetrackphilosopher.com/2019/07/21/beatles-career-kick-started-bet-winning-horse/.

"The Beatles Drop T Logo." The Beatles Bible, April 7, 2008. www.beatlesbible.com/features/drop-t-logo.

"Beatles Notebook Set for Sale in London." *New York Times*, August 7, 1998.

Bergen, Jay. *Lennon, the Mobster & the Lawyer: The Untold Story*. Memphis: Devault Graves Books, 2021.

Berkenstadt, Jim. *The Beatle Who Vanished*. Madison, WI: Rock and Roll Detective, 2013.

Bertram, Colin. "Inside John Lennon's 'Lost Weekend' Period." *Biography*, April 5, 2019 (updated June 1, 2020).

Best, Roag, with Pete Best and Rory Best. *The Beatles: The True Beginnings*. New York: Thomas Dunne Books, 2003.

Big Seven Music Corp. v. Lennon, 409 F. Supp. 122 (S. Dist. NY, February 20, 1976).

Big Seven Music Corp. v. Lennon, 554 F.2d 504 (US Ct. App., 2d Cir., April 13, 1977).

Bilyeau, Nancy. "The Night Elvis Met the Beatles." Medium, June 29, 2019.

Bishop, Moe. "Christmas Weirdness with the Beatles." Vice, December 21, 2011.

Black, Johnny. "The Rolling Stones: How It Happened." *The Online Library of Music Journalism*, 1995. https://teachrock.org/article/the-rolling-stones-how-it-happened/.

Bosso, Joe. "Andrew Loog Oldham: The Mastermind of the Rolling Stones." MusicRadar, January 2, 2013.

Brittain, Amy, "The Mobster's Son and the Pot Clinic: A Feud Grows in Jersey." *Star Ledger*, September 23, 2012.

Brown, Mick. "The Mystery of David Jacobs, the Liberace Lawyer." *The Telegraph*, June 3, 2013.

Burrows, Terry. *The Beatles Day by Day*. London: Chartwell Books, 2013.

Cambridge OneStop. 2011. *Morris Levy Interview 1986*. Video file. https://www.youtube.com/watch?v=DCdMCWzmMXQ.

Capozzi, Joe. "John Lennon's Last Years in Palm Beach." *Palm Beach Post*, November 1, 2018.

Cook, Craig. "Meet Jimmy Nicol, the Forgotten Beatle, Stand-In Drummer for Ringo." *The Advertiser*, June 11, 2014.

Crandall, Bill. "Motown Really Had a Hold on the Beatles." *CBS New York*, January 24, 2014.

Daley, Lauren. "From His Former Lover, a Quieter Portrait of Lennon during His 'Lost Weekend.'" *Boston Globe*, August 3, 2017.

Demain, Bill. "All Together Now: Civil Rights and the Beatles' First American Tour." *Mental Floss*, April 18, 2012.

Deriso, Nick. "Revisiting George Harrison's Ill-Fated 1974 North American Tour." *Ultimate Classic Rock*, November 2, 2015.

Deriso, Nick. "Why John Lennon and Paul McCartney's Final Session Was a Bust." *Ultimate Classic Rock*, March 28, 2016.

Diaz, Jesus. "How the Beatles Got Their Famous Logo." *Fast Company*, October 11, 2018.

Doggett, Peter. *You Never Give Me Your Money: The Beatles after the Breakup.* New York: Random House, 2009.

Dormehl, Luke. "Today in Apple History: Apple Goes to War with the Beatles Again." Cult of Mac, March 30, 2020.

Douglas, Lynn. "John Lennon and the Beatles Made a Painting Together, Now It's Up for Auction." *Forbes*, August 29, 2012.

Doyle, Jack. "Burn the Beatles, 1966: Bigger Than Jesus?" Pop History Dig, October 11, 2017.

Edwards, Gavin. "Beatles' 5 Boldest Rip-Offs." *Rolling Stone*, December 23, 2015.

Egan, Sean. "John Lennon Rock 'n' Roll Review." BBC, 2010.

Elsas, Dennis. "Andrew Loog Oldham—the Rolling Stones." October 2012 interview, DennisElsas.com.

Evans, Rush. "Q&A: Pete Best Looks Back on the Beginnings of the Fab Four." *Goldmine Magazine*, April 21, 2010.

"Ex-Beatle Tells How Black Stars Changed His Life." *Jet Magazine*, October 26, 1972.

Farber, Dan. "Tim Cook Maintains Steve Jobs' Beatles Business Model." CNET, June 12, 2013.

Fricke, David. "Gerry and the Pacemakers: Where Are They Now?" *Rolling Stone*, September 11, 1986.

Gabriele, Tony. "The Beatles Killed Irving Berlin?" *Daily Press*, June 11, 1996.

Giles, Jeff. "The Day Beatles Assistant Mal Evans Was Killed by Police." Ultimate Classic Rock, January 5, 2016.

Goodman, Fred. *Allen Klein—the Man Who Bailed Out the Beatles, Made the Stones, and Transformed Rock and Roll.* Boston: Mariner Books, 2015.

Greathouse, John. "This Rookie Mistake Cost the Beatles $100,000,000." *Forbes*, July 25, 2015.

Gunderson, Chuck. "The Untold Story of the Beatles' Desegregation Rider." *Culture Sonar*, July 31, 2020.

Gunderson, Chuck. *Some Fun Tonight—the Backstage Story of How the Beatles Rocked America.* San Diego, CA: Gunderson Media, 2013.

Hannum, Susan. "Portraits—Andy White." *Modern Drummer Magazine*, June 1986.

Havers, Richard. "I Wanna Be Your Man: When the Beatles Wrote for the Rolling Stones." uDiscover Music, November 16, 2020.

Havers, Richard. "Rock 'n' Roll: When John Lennon Returned to His Roots." uDiscover Music, February 18, 2020.

Hongo, Jun. "Paul McCartney Gets Back to the Budokan." *Wall Street Journal*, May 12, 2014.

Imagine Entertainment. *Eight Days a Week: The Touring Years.* Imagine Entertainment, 2016.

"Images of a Woman." *Born Late Blog*, June 18, 2011.

James, Tommy. *Me, the Mob and the Music: One Helluva Ride with Tommy James and the Shondells.* New York: Scribner, 2010.

Jolly, Nathan. "The History of Music Merch." Nathan Jolly's Geocities Site, February 10, 2016.

Jones, Josh. "The Last Time Lennon & McCartney Played Together Captured in *A Toot and a Snore in '74*." Open Culture, March 6, 2014.

Kane, Larry. *Ticket to Ride—Inside the Beatles 1964 World Tour That Changed the World.* Philadelphia: Running Press Book, 2003.

Knublauch, Thorsten. "Hamburg: Bambi Kino." *Kenwood Blog*, December 2, 2014. http://kenwoodlennon.blogspot.com/2014/12/hamburg-bambi-kino.html.

Kogon, Sam. "Andrew Loog Oldham Interview." Bandcamp, March 19, 2012.

Korkis, Jim. "Walt Disney World Chronicles: Nixon and the Beatles." *All Ears*, March 7, 2017.

Kozinn, Allan. "A Fond Look at Lennon's 'Lost Weekend.'" *New York Times*, March 12, 2008.

Kozinn, Allan. "Andy White, Drummer on the Beatles' Love Me Do, Dies at 85." *New York Times*, November 13, 2015.

Kreps, Daniel. "Andy White, Beatles 'Love Me Do' Drummer, Dead at 85." *Rolling Stone*, November 11, 2015.

Laney, Karen. "John Lennon Officially Ended the Beatles at Disney World." Ultimate Classic Rock, September 25, 2011.

Leafe, David. "Mona Best Gave the Fab Four Their Break." *Daily Mail*, December 12, 2018.

Lee, John. "Receiver Named for the Beatles." *New York Times*, March 13, 1971.

Lee, Peter. "The Mal Evans Diaries." Hooks and Harmony, August 10, 2009.

Leece, William. "Rory Storm: A Bright Future That Ended All Too Soon." *Liverpool Echo*, May 7, 2013.

Lennon, Cynthia. *John*. New York: Three Rivers, 2005.

Lewisohn, Mark. *All These Years, Volume 1: Tune In, Extended Special Edition*. London: Little, Brown UK, 2013.

Lewisohn, Mark. *The Complete Beatles Recording Sessions*. New York: Sterling, 1988.

Lindquist, David. "Beatles Drum Head Is Jim Irsay's Latest Purchase." *IndyStar*, November 10, 2015.

Littlejohn, Richard. "John Lennon Said He'd Thump Me If I Kept Churning Out Hits." *Daily Mail*, September 20, 2020.

"Love Me Do History." Beatles Music History, August 3, 2020. www.beatlesebooks.com./love-me-do.

Lozano, Carlos. "Grammy Winner Harry Nilsson Dies: Music: Singer-Songwriter, 52, Apparently Suffered a Heart Attack." *Los Angeles Times*, January 16, 1994.

Mariano, Kristen. "Reminiscing John Lennon's Last Four Summers in Karuizawa." *Travel Daily Media*, October 21, 2019.

Mastropolo, Frank. "13 Days as a Beatle: The Sad History of Jimmie Nicol." Ultimate Classic Rock, June 3, 2015.

Mastropolo, Frank. "John Lennon's Infamous 'Lost Weekend' Revisited." Ultimate Classic Rock, April 2. 2014.

McCartney, Paul. *The Lyrics: 1956 to the Present*. New York: Liveright, 2021.

McClure, Steve. "Yesterday—When the Beatles Typhoon Hit Japan." *Japan Times*, July 12, 2020.

McCoy, William, and Mitch Geary. "John Lennon: The Roots of Rock and Roll." RareBeatles.

Mellin, Joshua. "A Primer on Paul McCartney's Complicated History with—and Triumphant Return to—Japan." *Flood Magazine*, November 14, 2018.

Miles, Barry. *Paul McCartney: Many Years from Now*. New York: Henry Holt, 1997.

Mirken, Bruce. "1964, Civil Rights—and the Beatles?" Greenlining Institute, September 11, 2013.

"Moneywise: Beatleggers Are Trying to Grab a Large Share of the Beatle Merchandising Boom." *New York Times*, February 17, 1964.

"Morris Levy Is Dead; Power in Recording and Club Owner." *New York Times*, May 23, 1990.

Mullen, Tom. "The Beatles: What Really Inspired Eleanor Rigby." BBC News, September 11, 2017.

Nabhan, Shilby. "Showdown at Budokan." *Japan Times*, July 2, 2006.

Nicholson, James. *Never Say Die: A Kentucky Colt, the Epsom Derby, and the Rise of the Modern Thoroughbred Industry*. Lexington: University Press of Kentucky, 2013.

NME Daily Gossip. "Paul McCartney Deported for Condom Incident." NME Daily Gossip, October 29, 2008. https://www.nme.com/news/music/daily-gossip-701-1326118.

Norman, Phillip. *Shout*. London: Pan Books, 1993.

Oldham, Andrew Loog. *Stoned*. New York: Vintage Books, 2004.

Pang, May. *Instamatic Karma*. New York: St. Martin's, 2008.

"Paul McCartney and Pete Best Are Arrested in Hamburg." The Beatles Bible, November 26, 2018. https://www.beatlesbible.com/1960/11/29/paul-mccartney-pete-best-arrested-hamburg/.

Peeno, Jeffrey. "John Lennon and Paul McCartney's Secret Cocaine-Fueled Final Recording." *Far Out Magazine*, September 27, 2020.

Pfanner, Eric. "Apple vs. Apple in Dispute over Trademark." *New York Times*, March 29, 2006.

Pregnall, Andrew, Jason Arquette, Allyson Manhart, and Helen Goggins, eds. *Welcome to the Beatles*. Blacksburg, VA: VT Publishing, 2018.

Roberts, Lura. "Apple vs. Apple: Long-Running Legal Dispute Delayed Beatles' iTunes Deal." *The Telegraph*, November 16, 2010.

Robinson, Lisa. *There Goes Gravity—a Life in Rock and Roll*. New York: Riverhead Books, 2014.

Salkever, Alex. "John, Paul, George, Ringo . . . and Steve?" *Business Week*, September 30, 2004.

Savage, Mark. "The Bittersweet Symphony Dispute Is Over." BBC News, May 23, 2019.

"Seltaeb, Nicky Byrne and the Beatles Merchandise." *Everything Flows*, June 19, 2018.

Shooting Review Board Report and Officer-Involved Shooting Report, Los Angeles Police Department, D.R. # 76-430 212, July 6, 1976.

Sisario, Ben. "Allen Klein Dies; Managed Music Legends." *New York Times*, July 4, 2009.

Sisario, Ben. "Apple Begins Selling Beatles Downloads." *New York Times*, November 16, 2010.

Smallwood, Karl. "Forgotten Beatle—the Story of Jimmie Nicol." Today I Found Out, February 11, 2016. https://www.todayifoundout.com/index.php/2016/02/beatle-two-weeks-story-jimmy-nicol/.

Smith, Caspar Llewellyn. "Why the Beatles Sealed the Digital Deal with iTunes." *The Guardian*, November 20, 2010.

Smithfield, Brad. "The Sad Story of Jimmie Nicol: The Guy Who Replaced Ringo Star and Lived as a Beatle for Two Weeks." The Vintage News, May 2, 2016.

Sommer, Tim. "Why the Brilliance of the Beatles Should Piss You Off." *The Observer*, December 8, 2015.

Soocher, Stan. *Baby You're a Rich Man: Suing the Beatles for Fun & Profit*. Lebanon, NH: ForeEdge, 2015.

Soocher, Stan. "Did Litigation Kill the Beatles?" *American Bar Association Journal*, May 1, 2016.

Spitz, Bob. *The Beatles: The Biography*. Boston: Little, Brown, 2005.

Spizer, Bruce. *The Beatles on Apple Records*. Chicago: 498 Productions, 2003.

Stevens, Carolyn. *Media, Culture and Social Change in Asia: The Beatles in Japan*. London: Routledge, 2018.

Swanson, Dave. "The Day the Rolling Stones Signed to Decca Records." Ultimate Classic Rock, May 5, 2013.

Sweeting, Adam, and Will Hodgkinson. "Not Fade Away." *The Guardian*, May 24, 2000.

Tatsuji Nagashima obituary. *Billboard*, May 29, 1999.

Teutsch, Austin. "Portraits: Jimmy Nicol." *Modern Drummer*, June 1986.

Terrill, Marshall. "Whatever Happened to Jimmie Nicol? *Daytrippin' Beatles Magazine*, February 24, 2013.

Tsioulcas, Anastasia. "Not Bitter, Just Sweet: The Rolling Stones Give Royalties to the Verve." NPR, May 23, 2019.

Utton, Dominic. "The Beatles Lost Millions Because of Brian Epstein's Blunders." *The Express*, August 23, 2017.

Vargas, Ignacio [Ignazio2693]. *Paul McCartney & John Lennon 1968 Full Interview*. Video file, September 27, 2009. https://www.youtube.com/watch?v=Qp0i90n0BP8.

Wawzenek, Bryan. "25 Years Ago: The Beatles' Apple Corps Reaches a New Settlement with Apple Computer." Ultimate Classic Rock, October 11, 2016.

Welch, Chris. "How Did He Do It?" *Record Collector Magazine*, January 26, 2015.

White, Francine. "Mitch Murray: Songster Who Turned Down the Beatles." *The JC*, September 4, 2017.

Willet, Hugh. "How the Beatles Reinterpreted Black Music." *We're History*, March 11, 2015.

Williamson, Clifford. "1966: The Beatles' Tumultuous World Tour." *BBC History Extra*, June 1, 2017.

Wilson, Bob. "A Look Back: The Lennon and McCartney Sessions—*Toot & a Snore in '74*." Live for Live Music, April 2, 2014. https://liveforlivemusic.com/features/lennon-mccartney-toot-and-a-snore-74/.

Wolman, David. "How a Painting by the Beatles Ended Up Stashed under a Bed for 20 Years." *The Atlantic*, September 6, 2012.

Womack, Kenneth. *Solid State: The Story of Abbey Road and the End of the Beatles*. Ithaca, NY: Cornell University Press, 2019.

Wyman, Bill. *Rolling with the Stones*. London: DK Publishing, 2002.

Wyman, Bill. *Stone Alone*. Boston: Da Capo, 1990.

INDEX